Motivation Theory and Practice For Preservice Teachers

M. Kay Alderman
The University of Akron

and

Margaret W. Cohen
The University of Missouri-St. Louis

Volume Editors

Published by

**CLEARINGHOUSE
ON TEACHER
EDUCATION**

American Association of Colleges for Teacher Education
One Dupont Circle, Suite 610, Washington, D.C.
20036

June 1985

371,146
M918

CITE AS:
Alderman, M. Kay and Cohen, Margaret W. (1985). *Motivation Theory and Practice for Preservice Teachers* (Teacher Education Monograph No. 4). Washington, D.C.: ERIC Clearinghouse on Teacher Education.

MANUSCRIPTS:
The ERIC Clearinghouse on Teacher Education invites individuals to submit proposals for writing monographs for the Teacher Education Monograph Series. Proposals must include:

1. A detailed manuscript proposal of not more than five pages
2. a 75-word summary to be used by reviewers for the initial screening and rating of each proposal
3. a vita
4. a writing sample

ORDERS:
The price for a single copy, including fourth class postage and handling is $7.50. For first class postage, add $.60 for each copy ordered. Orders must be prepaid.

Library of Congress Catalog Card No.: 85-80315

ISBN 0-89333-037-X

ERIC CLEARINGHOUSE ON TEACHER EDUCATION
American Association of Colleges for Teacher Education
One Dupont Circle, NW, Suite 610
Washington, D.C. 20036
(202) 293-2450

Series Editor: Elizabeth A. Ashburn, Director, ERIC Clearinghouse on Teacher Education. Dr. Ashburn also serves as Director of Research and Information Services for the American Association of Colleges for Teacher Education.

This publication was prepared with funding from the National Institute of Education, U.S. Department of Education, under Contract No. 400-83-0022. The opinions expressed in this report do not necessarily reflect the positions or policies of NIE or DOE.

Contents

Acknowledgments

This monograph includes contributions from five authors who originally brought their work together in a symposium presented at the 1984 annual meeting of the American Educational Research Association (AERA) in New Orleans. The symposium was entitled "Essential Motivational Knowledge for the Preservice Teacher." Each author is actively engaged in research on motivation and involved in the teacher preparation program at his or her respective institution. We are delighted to see our commitments to both fields acknowledged with this publication.

A compendium like this one naturally requires the work of many people. Our thanks are due to the following:

To the departmental support staff at our universities, we offer thanks for their help in seeing us through several manuscript revisions.

To the anonymous AERA reviewers from the Teacher Preparation Curriculum Special Interest Group who initially offered us the opportunity to present our collaborative effort.

To Dr. Thomas L. Good, from the University of Missouri-Columbia, who served as discussant for our symposium at the AERA meeting and gave us the confidence to pursue our work together.

To the anonymous reviewers, selected by the ERIC Clearinghouse on Teacher Education, who enthusiastically received the manuscript.

To Dr. Elizabeth Ashburn, Director of the Clearinghouse, who efficiently guided us through the entire process of review and publication. We thank her for her interest, alacrity, and support.

To Francie Gilman and Celia Finstad, also at the Clearinghouse, who helped in various aspects of the review and editing phases of the project.

We have appreciated the help we have received and hope that this volume will be helpful to teacher educators and practitioners.

I

Introduction: Motivation As A Teaching Tool

M. Kay Alderman and Margaret W. Cohen

*The University of Akron and the University of
Missouri-St. Louis*

Knowledge about the relationship of motivation to learning has greatly increased in the last decade due to the expansion of motivation research into new areas. Research on extrinsic reinforcers, teacher and student attributions, and the social comparison process has extended understanding in ways that are particularly relevant for the preservice teacher. At the same time, successful motivation change programs pioneered by theorists such as McClelland and Winter (1971) and deCharms (1976) have been largely ignored in the teacher preparation curriculum. The articles in this volume grew out of a concern of the authors that although the motivational knowledge base has expanded, much of this new information has not been compiled in a way that it can be disseminated to preservice teachers. Thus, it is intended that this volume serve as a resource for teacher educators to approach the topic of motivation in a variety of courses.

The expanded knowledge base in motivation research is particularly important because it will enable teachers to play a more proactive role in the motivation of students than they previously have. The need for such a role is suggested by specialists in both motivation and research on teaching. From a motivational point of view, Nicholls (1979) asserts that optimum student motivation is a justifiable educational goal, but, at the same time, motivational inequality is pervasive in today's classrooms. Students who are motivated to work on their own and persist in tasks have an edge over those who do not. Thus, cognitive goals alone are insufficient for attaining equality in education. Nicholls further argues that we have done little so far to help teachers identify learner behaviors indicative of optimal motivation or to provide teachers with strategies for enhancing student motivation. Brophy (1983b), in a similar vein, suggests that developing motivation to learn in school is possible, and further, that it is important because increasing motivation should lead to improved learning. Thus, motivational knowledge for preservice teachers should include strategies that will help them motivate their students to accomplish academic tasks and work independently.

Marx and Winne (1983) believe that strategies for motivational change should be taught to all preservice teachers. As teachers, they, in turn, will teach "motivational sets" to their students. Specific motivational strategies identified as important for competent teaching are personal agency and attribution (Marx & Winne, 1983), and goal setting and self-management (Brophy, 1983a). In addition, the work by Ashton (1983, 1984) reveals that a teacher's sense of efficacy—that is, the extent to which teachers believe they have the capacity to affect student performance—is related to teaching practices. If preservice teachers are to become competent in fostering "motivational sets," the topics traditionally taught in the preservice curriculum are no longer adequate to prepare them. The field encompasses much more than Maslow's hierarchy of needs (1970) and various approaches to behavior modification.

The articles in this volume were originally developed as papers for a symposium presented at the 1984 annual meeting of the American Educational Research Association (AERA) to fill a perceived void in the motivational knowledge base in the teacher preparation curriculum. The material in these articles is more than additional theory to add to the instructional core for preservice teachers. Each of the authors suggests ways in which teachers can actively mediate to enhance student motivation.

Margaret W. Cohen, in the first article, reviews a body of research and theory concerned with the effects of extrinsic reinforcers on intrinsic motivation. She observes that although reinforcement has been regarded by many teachers and preservice teachers as the primary tool to achieve the classroom goals of management and instruction, the maintaining of positive classroom behaviors is not synonymous with intrinsically motivated learning. Cohen notes that contemporary research in the area of intrinsic motivation, such as that reported by Deci, Condry, Lepper and Greene, and McGraw, has consistently demonstrated that extrinsic reinforcers may undermine rather than facilitate performance on and interest in activities that are intrinsically motivating. She believes teacher educators need to be informed of this research and she derives guidelines for practitioners in the use of reinforcements.

Carole Ames integrates the research of Weiner, Ames, Nicholls, and Covington and Beery to address the implications of attribution theory for the teacher preparation curriculum. She observes that attribution research has focused on many of the problems teachers must deal with in the classroom—for example, how children develop a self-concept of ability, why students engage in failure avoidance behavior, when students value ability more than effort. Based on this body of research, Ames believes it is important for teacher educators to help preservice teachers understand the positive and negative effects of types of classroom structure and evaluation on attribution. Such knowledge helps teachers arrange classroom environments to enhance positive motivational states such as self-concept of ability.

Dale H. Schunk, in the context of self-efficacy theory, has been researching the motivational area of social comparison by integrating the work of Festinger with the research of theorists like Bandura and Veroff. He suggests that social comparison is an inherent factor in every classroom and can have positive or negative motivation effects. Schunk stresses that preservice teachers need to be aware of educational practices such as rewards, modeling, and tutoring that can affect student social comparisons. He observes that developmental differences need to be taken into account in making comparative evaluations and teachers need to be able to assess how age groups differ. Schunk also notes that an understanding of the social comparison processes is needed by preservice teachers to enable them to design classroom activities and give effective feedback.

M. Kay Alderman, in her article, contends that although achievement motivation theory has been the focus of much research since the 1950s, its potential applicability for enhancing motivation has not been tapped. Based on the work of such researchers as Good, Brophy and Evertson, and Brookover et al., Alderman has identified characteristics of successful teachers that are similar to the characteristics of persons with high needs for achievement identified by McClelland and Winter, and deCharms. She suggests that the preservice component in motivation should provide the preservice teacher with a repertoire of motivation-linked strategies such as goal-setting in order to facilitate learning and to educate students with high-achievement patterns of thought and action.

Mary Rohrkemper, like Alderman, argues that theoretical knowledge of motivational research and theory is not sufficient. Drawing from the research on teacher effectiveness and decision making generated by theorists like Good and Brophy, Morine-Dershimer, and Shavelson, Rohrkemper argues that if preservice teachers are to be adequately prepared, they need concrete skills that will enable them to observe motivation, diagnose the need for motivational strategies, and assess the effectiveness of strategy implementation. Rohrkemper also differentiates between proactive (decisions and behavior prior to instruction) and reactive (decisions and behavior that occur during instruction) motivational strategies and describes how observation and interviewing skills can be incorporated into the teacher preparation curriculum.

In summary, these authors propose expanding the topic of motivation in the preservice education program by including contemporary research. The articles included in this volume clearly establish that there is a body of research available to help prepare teachers to understand and to promote student motivation. The task of compiling and interpreting current motivational research, however, entails relying on the psychological theories that generated it. As with most topics in psychology, each theory brings with it a corresponding set of terminology. This is the case also with the articles in this volume. The field of motivation is extensive and so is its language. Each researcher within the field is guided by a particular theory which explains some aspect of why individuals behave. The strength of motivational research lies in the fact that it is grounded in such theory. Despite the fact that the language of each theory differs, the common theme of improving teacher and student motivation remains. It is the authors' intent that by means of this volume teacher educators will learn a new language to help them describe motivation both more precisely and extensively. Change involves wanting to learn. Wanting to learn is motivation. It is our hope that teacher educators will use this volume with the same fervor that they want their preservice teachers to bring to the classroom.

References

Ashton, P. (1983). *A study of teachers' sense of efficacy.* Final report, executive summary. Gainesville, FL: University of Florida. (ERIC Document Reproduction Service No. ED 231 833)

Ashton, P. (1984). Teacher efficacy: A motivational paradigm for effective teacher education. *Journal of Teacher Education, 35,* 28–32.

Brookover, W., Beady, C., Flood, P., Schweitzer, J., & Wisenbaker, J. (1979). *School social systems and student achievement.* New York: Praeger.

Brophy, J. (1983a). Classroom organization and management. *Elementary School Journal, 83* (4), 265–285 (ERIC No. EJ 281 535)

Brophy, J. (1983b). Conceptualizing student motivation. *Educational Psychologist, 18,* 200–215.

deCharms, R. (1976). *Enhancing motivation.* New York: Irvington/Wiley.

McClelland, D. C., & Winter, D. G. (1971). *Motivating economic achievement.* New York: Free Press.

Marx, R. W., & Winne, P. H. (1983, April). Knowledge and skills teachers need to influence students' cognitive learning. Paper presentation at annual meeting of the American Educational Research Association, Montreal, Quebec.

Nicholls, J. (1979). Quality and equality in intellectual development: The role of motivation in education. *American Psychologist, 34,* 1071–1084. (ERIC No. EJ 218 804)

II

Extrinsic Reinforcers and Intrinsic Motivation

Margaret W. Cohen

University of Missouri-St. Louis

Until recently the topic of intrinsic motivation was narrowly addressed in the undergraduate teacher education curriculum. Approaches to maintaining discipline in the classroom by applying principles derived from learning theories were considered within the scope of motivation, along with the classic work of psychologists like Maslow (1954), Murray (1938), and White (1959). Fortunately, these shortcomings are being redressed as contemporary authors surveying topics within educational psychology incorporate into their manuscripts theoretical advances in the field of intrinsic motivation.

An approach which has been consistently emphasized in the teacher training curriculum is that of applied behavior analysis. Preservice teachers are taught to rely on principles of extrinsic reinforcement to manage classroom behaviors and to enhance the instructional process. Maintaining positive classroom behaviors, however, is not synonymous with intrinsically motivating learning. Not only do teachers need to learn about alternatives for motivating students, but they should also be informed of current research which raises questions about the relationship of extrinsic reinforcement and intrinsic motivation. The former topic, alternative approaches to motivation, is being addressed by the other contributors to this volume. The latter subject, the effects of extrinsic reinforcers on intrinsic motivation, is the focus of this discussion.

CAUTIONS RELATED TO EXTRINSIC REINFORCEMENT

The judicious use of reinforcement is emphasized during teacher training. Preservice teachers are encouraged to present their students with intangible rewards like praise, attention, positive feedback, and if necessary, tangible rewards such as tokens, gold stars, and check-marks. Preservice teachers learn to distinguish positive reinforcement from negative reinforcement and punishment, and are encouraged to structure contingencies using the positive options. Here the first problem arises in teaching behavior modification; there is confusion over the difference between reward and reinforcement. The consequences of teacher intervention can be labeled reinforcing only if there is an increase in learners' subsequent behaviors. If not, rewards cannot be said to be reinforcing and may, in fact, have an undesirable effect on behavior.

Of those teachers who do collect data and verify that reinforced behaviors actually increase, many will lose sight of the long-term objectives of using applied behavior analysis. The teacher has two choices in administering reinforcements regularly. On the one hand, schedules can be developed and implemented so that rewards are eventually phased out, with students receiving infrequent intermittent reinforcement by the conclusion of the program. Alternatively, during the course of the modification process, students can learn how to arrange their reinforcement contingencies so that they are managing their own behaviors by deciding, for example, how many credits toward free time they can earn by completing so many assignments. In either case, teachers' responsible use of these behavioral tools requires fading out reinforcers and, concomitantly, moving from the use of tangible to intangible reinforcers. Even when these procedures are followed, learners remain under the control of environmental contingencies. It cannot be said that they are intrinsically motivated so long as the response to the question "why are you performing?" remains "in order to attain a reinforcer, the teacher's approval, or a high grade, etc."

Perhaps the most important guideline to rely upon when contemplating the use of reinforcement is the axiom that behavior modification is designed to teach new behaviors or to increase behaviors which occur with low probability. Otherwise, the effects of using reinforcement can actually diminish the frequency of behavior or undermine students' existing motivation to perform. For behavioral techniques to be administered accurately and with integrity, they must be applied as part of a carefully formulated program. A difficulty here is that each teacher preparation curriculum may not address all the complexities involved in training educators in applied behavior analysis. Consequently, reinforcement may be inadvertently misused. Counsel as to how to avoid potential misapplications comes from one recent avenue of research on intrinsic motivation.

INTRINSIC MOTIVATION

In contrast to the extrinsic response to the question of "why are you performing?", responses indicative of intrinsic motivation acknowledge the important role of an individual's experiences, perceptions, and emotions with explanations such as "I enjoy doing X" or "I want to accomplish Y." Elements of cognition and affect are regarded as integral aspects of theories of intrinsic motivation. Individual perceptions and capabilities are taken into account in the work of researchers like Condry (1978), Condry and Chambers (1978), Deci (1975, 1980), Lepper (1983), Lepper and Greene (1978), and McGraw (1978), who have advanced practitioners' understanding of how reinforcement can help or hinder the process of learning. The results of this research can sharpen preservice teachers' knowledge of how to manage students' behaviors effectively and how to structure curricula more efficiently.

The "Overjustification" Hypothesis

Lepper and Greene's (1978) and Lepper's (1983) research is designed to test the hypothesis that intrinsic interest in an activity will decrease if inducements to engage in the activity in order to attain an incentive are provided. The hypothesis assumes initial intrinsic interest in the task and predicts that if the justification or incentive offered for the activity is beyond that which the task would provide in-and-of itself, the person will perceive the activity as a means to attaining that incentive. The incentive, therefore, provides overjustification for task engagement.

Tests of the hypothesis have consistently demonstrated that when rewards are offered to engage in a task that a person already finds interesting, the subject's subsequent interest in performing the task will decrease. This effect has been found with preschoolers (Greene & Lepper, 1974), fourth graders (Boggiano & Ruble, 1979; Greene & Lepper, 1974), high school students (Kruglanski, Friedman, & Zeevi, 1971), and college-aged and adult populations (Deci, 1971, 1972, 1975; Pittman, Cooper, & Smith, 1977). The pattern prevails also when negative reinforcement has been used (Lepper, 1973). These findings clearly indicate that when students show an interest in an activity, not only are rewards superfluous, but they can also distort learners' perceptions of why they are engaged in a task.

A qualifying issue requiring clarification deals with whether the rewards are administered contingently or noncontingently on task performance. Decrements in subsequent intrinsic interest will only be apparent if the learner perceived the initial link between the activity and the reward as constraining (Lepper & Greene, 1978). In situations where a prize or reward was unexpectedly given (noncontingent), the results of research testing the overjustification hypothesis do not show diminished intrinsic interest (Lepper, Greene, & Nisbett, 1973) because the learner had no prior expectation of a reward. Caution must be used in generalizing these findings to the classroom, however, since the studies assess intrinsic interest only once after the experimental manipulation. In the classroom

8

setting the later presence of a teacher who is associated with dispensing rewards (even if rewards were previously noncontingent) may certainly influence the learner's reasons for and interest in engaging in the activity.

The relationship between contingent rewards and subsequent intrinsic interest is also apparent in other instances where learners perceive their environments as constraining. A deadline imposed upon an initially interesting task (Amabile, DeJong, & Lepper, 1976) or surveillance by an adult (Lepper & Greene, 1975) have been demonstrated to lead to diminished interest. Teachers routinely observe students' performances and impose due dates for assignments. To the extent that students believe these actions to be limiting, there is danger that their future motivation to do similar activities will not be intrinsic. This admonition is clarified and confirmed with Deci's (1975, 1980) contributions to the area.

Cognitive Evaluation Theory

Deci (1978) and Deci and Porac (1978) refer to intrinsic motivation as activity "in which people *seek out and conquer challenges that are optimal for their capabilities*" (p. 151). People seek challenges because meeting them fulfills an intrinsic need to be competent and self-determining. If meeting such challenges is rewarded, individuals' perceptions of why they are pursuing their goals may change. Cognitive evaluation theory accounts for these changes by postulating that a person's locus of causality for engaging in the behavior changes from an internal to an external locus. Numerous studies (compiled in Deci, 1975) verified the findings of Lepper and Greene (1978) discussed earlier that when rewards are contingent on performing an intrinsically interesting activity, they will change a person's perception of where the locus of causality lies.

The basic premise of Deci's approach, that we act to experience competence and self-determination, led Deci to question whether all rewards diminish intrinsic motivation for all individuals. Subsequent research investigating the impact of positive and negative verbal feedback on the intrinsic motivation of male and female subjects revealed complex patterns of heightened or diminished motivation (Deci, 1971, 1972, 1978; Deci & Porac, 1978). Deci postulates that rewards can be used either to control or to inform persons about their competence and self-determination. Therefore, the effects of the rewards are dependent not only on the recipient's perception and interpretation of them, but also by the intention and manner of the administrator. Students who believe a tangible reward or praise is controlling them will lose interest in the task. Their locus of causality will be external. Students who use the feedback to give themselves information about their progress and performance will have enhanced interest in the task and their locus of causality will remain internal.

9

The theoretical implications for classroom practice are clear. In a practical sense, the findings call for a great deal of sensitivity on the teacher's part. Preservice teachers must learn to use informational rewards to let students know that they are competent. They must learn to avoid using rewards to control students' behaviors or which convey that the purpose of the task is inherent in the reward itself. This calls into question the language teachers routinely use to dispense feedback. "I like the way you are ... attending or solving the problem or participating" communicates control because it conveys that the student is behaving to please the teacher, rather than to satisfy his or her intrinsic need to be competent and self-determining. Informational feedback places the responsibility and ownership of the behavior on the student in a manner that gives the learner autonomy.

Teacher educators and practitioners should rethink the manner in which they deliver feedback so that the credit for the performance belongs to the learner. Phrases such as "you can be proud of your presentation" and "that was exceptional reasoning" give students specific information about their contributions. An additional impetus to incorporate these findings into the teacher preparation curriculum comes from Deci, Nezlek and Scheinman (1981), who found that children taught by teachers with an informing or autonomous orientation were more intrinsically motivated and had higher self-esteem than children taught by teachers with a controlling orientation.

The Task and Its Context

In contrast to Deci's and Lepper and Greene's attention to different types of incentives and how they are administered, McGraw's (1978) research has emphasized the nature of the activity by postulating that rewards will differentially affect learners, depending on both the structure and attractiveness of the activity. McGraw classifies tasks along two dimensions: whether they are perceived as attractive or aversive and whether their solutions are algorithmic or heuristic. His review of studies demonstrating increased or diminished intrinsic motivation reveals that these two dimensions can account for the effect extrinsic incentives will have on performance.

The attractive-aversive dimension is dependent on the learner's perception of the task as intrinsically interesting versus unchallenging and odious. The algorithmic-heuristic dimension refers to whether task solutions involve either applying established formulas to arrive at convergent solutions or using problem-solving skills to arrive at divergent solutions. Although some algorithmic procedures are derived from heuristic processes and tasks vary on an attractiveness continuum, for purposes of explication it is simpler to regard the two dimensions as a two-by-two matrix.

10

Tasks which are algorithmic and aversive generally involve memorization and rote learning. Rewards can facilitate this type of learning because there is no other source of motivation present. Algorithmic and attractive tasks challenge learners to apply a previously learned formula. Assuming students enjoy the task and know how to apply its algorithm, McGraw and McCullers (cited in McGraw, 1978) found that rewards for correct solutions can facilitate task performance. Rewards encourage correct performance and may provide students with a rationale for exerting more effort.

Heuristic activities are inherently engaging and interesting, so it is difficult to conceptualize an aversive, heuristic activity. McGraw suggests that a heuristic activity may be unattractive to a tired or sick student and that rewards may facilitate learning in such cases. Although there presently is no empirical support for this hypothesis, its rationale strengthens the admonishment that teachers be attentive to individual differences between learners both in terms of their perceptions of the tasks and their affective states during performance.

The combination of attractive tasks with heuristic solutions refers to problem solving and creative activity evident most often during independent learning. Research in this area has concentrated on the use of classic, functional fixedness problems in which the successful problem solution is dependent on the learner using novel applications of previously learned or perceived relationships. McGraw's review demonstrates that here rewards can have a detrimental impact by hampering the creative process. Analogous classroom activities must encourage divergent thinking and discovery and be attractive to students.

Condry (1978) and Condry and Chambers (1978) offer another explanation for why rewards detract from the process of learning in situations which involve attractive, heuristic tasks. These studies demonstrate that rewards, rather than undermining motivation, alter the motivational locus of the activity from an intrinsic to an extrinsic context. The intrinsic context places emphasis on the activity and progress toward its completion. Tasks are engaged in by choice and selected because they are challenging and focus the learner on integrating information. Learning which occurs in the extrinsic context places an emphasis on performance and not the activities involved in learning. The element of choice is absent and task engagement occurs due to the anticipation of receiving rewards. Learners will be less interested in resuming a task completed within an extrinsic, compared to an intrinsic, context because they have avoided involvement and engagement in the activity. Should incentives be introduced to the intrinsic context, they will alter the motivational context to an extrinsic one, and consequently diminish performance on heuristic and attractive tasks.

11

Condry's motivational contexts are similar to deCharms' (1968, 1976) concepts of origin and pawn. When ownership of a task is removed from a learner by the teacher or by a reward, the student, who initiated the activity and experienced feelings of origination and control, may now be placed in the role of a pawn in the environment. Solutions to open-ended, heuristic problems need to be owned by the learner for intrinsic motivation to be enhanced. Condry (1978) provides a theoretical explanation and empirical data to support McGraw's (1978) observation that ownership can be removed by extrinsic incentives. Condry's further concern is that environments must be arranged to enhance the processes of learning and discovery of the intrinsic context.

DISCUSSION

When, then, is it appropriate for teachers to use extrinsic incentives? An important difference between the research on the detrimental effects of rewards and the traditional, behavioral use of reinforcers reflects one basic distinction between the applications of behavioral and cognitive psychology. Management of student behaviors is quite different from the instructional processes that take into account students' interests, capabilities, and perceptions. In order to acquire knowledge (cognition), students must know how to sit still and attend to their teacher (behavior). It may be that the judicious use of reinforcers applies mostly to helping students acquire behaviors necessary for learning, and only somewhat to certain types of instructional activities. In either case, preservice teachers need to learn how to attend to the individual differences between their students in order to assess what the potential impact of rewards will be on each, given the behavioral or instructional circumstances. This entails knowledge of the research regarding the appropriate use of reinforcers and inappropriate use of rewards. Both Deci (1978) and deCharms (1983) have summarized the implications of the research reviewed in this presentation into guidelines which can challenge and direct practitioners. These are:

1. When rewards are unnecessary because students already know how to engage in the behavior, they should not be used.
2. When rewards are unnecessary because students find the instructional activity interesting, they should not be used.
3. When rewards are introduced to control students' behaviors or to control students' reasons for engaging in instructional activities, they should not be used.
4. When instructional activities involve students' creativity and emphasize divergent thinking and problem solving, rewards should not be used.

12

5. When reinforcers are introduced to provide students with information about their competence or to help them accomplish an instructional activity, rewards will facilitate intrinsic motivation.
6. When instructional activities involve memorization, convergent thinking, applying formulas, and using well-learned skills, reinforcers will facilitate performance.

Expanding research in the area of motivation is providing educators with new insights into the psychology of learning and, specifically, into the correlation between rewards and performance. Preservice teachers need to be apprised of the possibly chilling effect of offering inducements for students to engage in intrinsically interesting work. Likewise, it is important to understand the types of tasks and situations where rewards will be effective and will facilitate learning. Teacher education curricula should include both the theoretical foundation and the practical guidelines to provide the beginning teacher with an appropriate and useful repertoire of motivational tools.

References

Amabile, T. M., DeJong, W., & Lepper, M. R. (1976). Effects of externally imposed deadlines on subsequent intrinsic motivation. *Journal of Personality and Social Psychology, 34,* 92–98.

Boggiano, A. K., & Ruble, D. N. (1979). Competence and the overjustification effect: A developmental study. *Journal of Personality and Social Psychology, 37,* 1462-1468. (ERIC No. EJ 219 985)

Condry, J. (1978). The role of incentives in socialization. In M. R. Lepper & D. Greene (Eds.), *The hidden costs of reward* (pp. 179–192). Hillsdale, NJ: Erlbaum.

Condry, J., & Chambers, J. (1978). Intrinsic motivation and the process of learning. In M. R. Lepper & D. Greene (Eds.), *The hidden costs of reward* (pp. 61–84). Hillsdale, NJ: Erlbaum.

deCharms, R. (1976). *Enhancing motivation: Change in the classroom.* New York: Irvington Publications.

deCharms, R. (1983). Intrinsic motivation, peer tutoring, and cooperative learning: Practical maxims. In J. M. Levine & M. C. Wang (Eds.), *Teacher and student perceptions: Implications for learning* (pp. 391–398). Hillsdale, NJ: Erlbaum.

deCharms, R. (1968). *Personal causation.* New York: Academic Press.

Deci, E. L. (1978). Applications of research on the effects of rewards. In M. R. Lepper & D. Greene (Eds.), *The hidden costs of reward* (pp. 149–176). Hillsdale, NJ: Erlbaum.

Deci, E. L. (1971). Effects of externally mediated rewards on intrinsic motivation. *Journal of Personality and Social Psychology, 18,* 105–115. (ERIC No. EJ 035 993)

Deci, E. L. (1975). *Intrinsic motivation.* New York: Plenum Press.

Deci, E. L. (1972). Intrinsic motivation, extrinsic reinforcement, and inequity. *Journal of Personality and Social Psychology, 22,* 113–120. (ERIC No. EJ 055 496)

Deci, E. L. (1980). *The psychology of self-determination.* Lexington, MA: D. C. Heath.

Deci, E. L., Nezlek, J., & Sheinman, L. (1981). Characteristics of the rewarder and intrinsic motivation of the rewardee. *Journal of Personality and Social Psychology, 40,* 1–10.

Deci, E. L., & Porac, J. (1978). Cognitive evaluation theory and the study of human motivation. In M. R. Lepper & D. Greene (Eds.), *The hidden costs of reward* (pp. 149–176). Hillsdale, NJ: Erlbaum.

Greene, D., & Lepper, M. R. (1974). Effects of extrinsic rewards on children's subsequent intrinsic interest. *Child Development, 45,* 1141–1145. (ERIC No. EJ 109 800)

Kruglanski, A. W., Friedman, I., & Zeevi, G. (1971). The effects of extrinsic incentives on some qualitative aspects of task performance. *Journal of Personality, 39*, 606–617.

Lepper, M. R. (1973). Dissonance, self-perception, and honesty in children. *Journal of Personality and Social Psychology, 25*, 65–74. (ERIC No. EJ 080 278)

Lepper, M. R. (1983). Extrinsic reward and intrinsic motivation: Implications for the classroom. In J. M. Levine & M. C. Wang (Eds.), *Teacher and student perceptions: Implications for learning* (pp. 281–317). Hillsdale, NJ: Erlbaum.

Lepper, M. R., & Greene, D. (1978). *The hidden costs of reward: New perspectives on the psychology of human motivation.* Hillsdale, NJ: Erlbaum.

Lepper, M. R., & Greene, D. (1975). Turning play into work: Effects of adult surveillance and extrinsic rewards on children's intrinsic motivation. *Journal of Personality and Social Psychology, 31*, 479–486.

Lepper, M. R., Greene, D., & Nisbitt, R. E. (1973). Undermining children's intrinsic interest with extrinsic rewards: A test of the "overjustification" hypothesis. *Journal of Personality and Social Psychology, 28*, 129–137. (ERIC No. EJ 085 275)

Maslow, A. H. (1954). *Motivation and personality.* New York: Harper & Row.

McGraw, K. O. (1978). The detrimental effects of reward on performance: A literature review and a prediction model. In M. R. Lepper & D. Greene (Eds.), *The hidden costs of reward* (pp. 33–60). Hillsdale, NJ: Erlbaum.

Murray, H. A. (1938). *Explorations in personality.* New York: Oxford.

Pittman, T. S., Cooper, E. E., & Smith, T. W. (1977). Attribution of causality and the overjustification effect. *Personality and Social Psychology Bulletin, 3*, 280–283.

White, R. W. (1959). Motivation reconsidered: The concept of competence. *Psychological Review, 66*, 297–333.

III

Attributions and Cognitions in Motivation Theory

Carole Ames

University of Illinois

Why do some students think success in school means to "get all the answers right" or "to get A's on your report card," while others attach more importance to "improving your work" or "trying your hardest," and even others to just "finishing the assignments?" When are teachers more likely to help a student rather than blame a student for his/her failure? Why do some classrooms create a perception of differences among students, while others foster perceptions of similarity? And finally, when can positive feedback from the teacher actually serve to undermine student motivation? Although there are a number of factors that are involved in considering the above questions, the issues they raise can be addressed from a cognitive motivational perspective.

MOTIVATION AND ATTRIBUTION

Motivation can be viewed as reflecting different ways of thinking. As suggested by Corno and Mandinach (1983), two students may be equally motivated to learn but may differ in how they think about themselves, how they think about the task, and how they think about the goal. Thus, on the one hand we may want students to persist longer, work harder, or spend more time on a task; on the other hand, we may be equally, if not more, concerned about getting students to focus on one set of information and not another, to value certain goals and objectives over others, to implement certain strategies when working on a task (Maehr, 1984). When motivation is construed in this manner, it can be seen as an outcome in itself. As a consequence, motivation and short-term achieve-

16

ment outcomes may not be directly related. While immediate achievement is determined by a variety of factors and success may even be assured in a number of ways, outcomes such as a willingness to learn, positive self-worth, and self-regulated learning involve a cognitive view of motivation. This cognitive view stands aside from traditional concepts such as energy, persistence, and time on task.

A study of achievement-related attributions provides one framework for examining motivational processes (Weiner, 1979). Attribution theory tells us how students and teachers assess or interpret the causes of achievement outcomes. While achievement outcomes can be attributed to a wide range of factors, the differentiation of ability and effort factors has received the most attention and carries the most implications for self-evaluation. Both ability and effort describe characteristics of the person, but they generally differ in perceived stability and controllability.

It is significant that some students believe that they have failed because of a lack of ability, while others believe that they didn't try hard enough or use the appropriate strategies. The latter students—those who ascribe failure to variable and controllable factors—have been labeled mastery or success-oriented, while those who ascribe failure to a lack of ability have been labeled as failure-avoiding and sometimes helpless. We can expect different patterns of coping with the academic environment from these students, specifically with regard to the likelihood that they will engage in further efforts to achieve or persist in the face of failure.

Research findings (Dweck, 1975) suggest that it is the success or mastery-oriented children who are more likely to engage in these behaviors. These mastery children hold *a priori* beliefs in the covariation of effort and achievement, and they also tend to become very strategy-focused when they experience failure. And, for children to be self-regulated learners, they need to be focused on strategies that can enhance their performance. These strategies might include general or specific cognitive approaches to planning or monitoring actions. In contrast, the helpless children tend to focus on their inadequacy following failure. Recent research (Ames, 1984a) shows that these same patterns of cognition (that is, a strategy as opposed to an ability focus) are elicited by different types of learning environments. The implication is that the structure of the classroom may actually educate these different motivational thought patterns.

Teacher Feedback

There are also age-related changes in the perceived relationship of ability and effort. Young children hold an incremental view of ability—that is, one gets smarter by trying harder (Nicholls & Jagacinski, 1983). Effort and ability are, in this way, correlated. Young children who are praised for

17

their effort tend to see themselves as capable. To the older child, adolescent, and adult, however, the person who succeeds without trying is smartest. In fact, there is even perceived value in not trying—success without trying presents a strong case that one is smart. In the case of failure, one's self-concept of ability is protected by not trying, a pattern which Covington and Beery (1976) describe as "failure with honor." For teachers, trying hard has value, and they tend to praise students who do try hard; for students, low effort has survival value. It provides a way to avoid ascriptions of low ability from one's peers as well as oneself and can serve to aggrandize one's ability following success.

Thus, praising older students for effort may be ineffective when students believe that ability is more important and valued. As highlighted by Brophy (1981) in a recent article, praise for something that only reflects what all or any student could do does not lead to personal attributions. When praise is given contingently and judiciously, however, students are more likely to make self-attributions of "something special" about oneself. Further, when reward is given for form, rather than substance, and criticism given for poor performance, success is likely to be attributed to external factors and failure to lack of ability. In a similar way, effective expressions of sympathy following student failure convey indirectly that the student is not capable. Teacher feedback is therefore a potent source for student self-attributions and inasmuch as the feedback is public, these self-attributions are even more powerful because they can be validated by peers.

Classroom Structures

In addition to direct teacher feedback, the structure of the classroom also influences student attributional patterns, particularly to the extent to which students focus on ability as opposed to effort (Ames, 1984b). Goal or reward structure is a social and evaluation dimension of the classroom environment, defining the way in which students are evaluated, as well as how they relate to each other and to the task. The research has traditionally focused on three types of goal structures—competitive, cooperative and individualistic; classrooms have also been differentiated more generally according to task structure, grouping practices, student autonomy, and method of evaluation.

A competitive structure is reflected in classroom practices such as using comparative criteria for grading, grouping by ability, publicly charting student progress, calling attention to students exhibiting exemplary behavior, games, etc. The imposition of social comparison in this structure focuses children on evaluating their own ability. By contrast, in individualistic structures children tend to be more concerned with their effort and task strategies. In fact, individualistic as opposed to competitive goal structures generate cognitions that reflect a differential mastery in con-

18

trast to a helpless orientation. Nicholls (1979) has labeled this phenomenon as a task-involved versus an ego-involved motivational state. In other words, children tend to question their own ability in competitive situations ("Am I smart?"), while those in an individualistic structure often focus on their effort ("Am I trying hard enough?") and on strategies for improving or maintaining their performance ("How can I do this?").

Competitive as opposed to individualistic goal structures also affect the way children attend to sources of performance information. In competitive situations children are focused on self-other comparisons; in individualistic settings, children pay attention to how they are performing now relative to how they performed in the past. The implication here is that while teachers may be interested in a child's performance over time, the instructor may have difficulty getting students to attend to this information if the uderlying structure of the classroom is competitive in nature.

Research also suggests that cooperative and competitive goal structures have markedly different effects on students' interpersonal perceptions. Whereas competition creates perceptions of sharp differences in levels of ability, cooperation tends to minimize these differences even when students' actual performances are markedly different. Perceptions of inequality arise in competitive environments, but perceptions of equality prevail in cooperative settings. Comparable feelings have also emerged from the study of teachers' evaluations of students. That is, teachers evaluations of high- and low-achieving students tend to be more divergent in competitive than cooperatively structured settings. Thus, the classroom structure can create a climate for differentiation or similarity, and these perceptions seem to be shared by teachers and students. The very structure the teacher creates can serve to undermine attempts to equalize motivational opportunities for students.

THE EDUCATOR'S ROLE IN DEVELOPING MOTIVATION

What can teachers do in the classroom to enhance motivation from an attribution perspective?

First, students who have a history of failure or those who believe that they have inadequate ability, may benefit from attribution retraining. Attribution change programs work through cueing and reinforcement (getting students to verbalize effort as a cause of their performance and reinforcing these verbalizations) to help students focus on the role of effort in their performance. The basic premise of such retraining is that these attributions mediate and are prerequisite to subsequent positive achievement actions. Two caveats to such an approach are that the task must be realistic—the goal must be attainable from the student's perspective such that reasonable effort will lead to success. Further, accomplishment of the goal must be seen by the student as reflecting both ability

19

and effort. According to Covington and Omelich (1979), students prefer to be seen as capable *and* hard working, while the teacher may be sufficiently satisfied when students are working hard. Thus, attribution change programs may need to build in rewards for trying—such as by providing incentives for effort or changing the instructional environment so that effort is perceived as valued.

Second, the social context of the classroom can influence children's thinking. The structure of the learning environment not only focuses children on different sources of performance information, but also contributes to different attributional patterns. While the educational literature has tended to take advocacy positions that pit one type of goal structure against another in relation to immediate achievement outcomes, this literature overlooks other psychological processes that are important to long-term learning and self-directed learning (Johnson & Johnson, 1975; Slavin, 1983). Thus, students may be socialized into specific attribution patterns as a function of the goal structure they experience over time.

Finally, recent research suggests that there may be a potential linkage between attributions and other types of student thoughts (Ames, 1984a). There is some indication that effort attributions may be linked to other cognitive activities that are directed toward monitoring and regulating learning. This strategy orientation is related to an individual's belief that achievement is effort-determined. In addition, strategies for learning are more likely to develop in the context of classroom structures which utilize an individualistic form of evaluation emphasizing self-improvement. This is not to say that a sense of personal responsibility will by itself assure the development of cognitive strategies, but the occurrence of effort attributions and strategies may be facilitated by the same external condition. If children are questioning their ability, they may not be able to become strategy-focused, and those conditions which contribute to an ability focus may block students from engaging in learning strategies and self-regulatory processes. Thus, the social context or structure of the classroom may support or undermine efforts to change individual thought processes.

In conclusion, it appears that educators may be able to alter the psychological meaning of success and failure through retraining programs, as well as by structuring of the learning environment. Moreover, it is important to remember that the benefits/detriments of different types of goal structures may not be evident by examining short-term achievement outcomes. The recent research indicates that instructional practices may socialize children into certain motivation patterns that may put them at a disadvantage in the classroom; furthermore, the structure of the classroom may affect teachers' perceptions/evaluations of students and influence instructional strategies.

20

References

Ames, C. (1984a). Achievement attributions and self-instruction under competitive and individualistic goal structures. *Journal of Educational Psychology, 76,* 478–487.

Ames, C. (1984b). Competitive and individualistic goal structures: A cognitive motivational analysis. In R. Ames & C. Ames (Eds.), *Research on motivation in education: Student motivation* (pp. 177–207). New York: Academic Press.

Brophy, J. (1981). Teacher praise: A functional analysis. *Review of Educational Research, 51,* 5–32. (ERIC No. EJ 246 420)

Corno, L., & Mandinach, E. (1983). The role of cognitive engagement in classroom learning and motivation. *Educational Psychologist, 18,* 88–108.

Covington, M., & Beery, R. (1976). *Self-worth and school learning.* New York: Holt, Rinehart, and Winston.

Covington, M., & Omelich, C. (1979). It's best to be able and virtuous, too: Student and teacher evaluative responses to successful effort. *Journal of Educational Psychology, 71,* 688–700. (ERIC No. EJ 218 634)

Dweck, C. S. (1975). The role of expectation and attribution in the alleviation of learned helplessness. *Journal of Personality and Social Psychology, 31,* 674–685.

Johnson, D. W., & Johnson, R. P. (1975). *Learning together and alone.* Englewood Cliffs, NJ: Prentice-Hall. (ERIC Document Reproduction Service No. ED 104 868)

Maehr, M. (1984). Meaning and motivation: Toward a theory of personal investment. In R. Ames & C. Ames (Eds.), *Research on motivation in education: Student motivation* (pp. 115–144). New York: Academic Press.

Nicholls, J. G. (1979). Quality and equality in intellectual development: The role of motivation in education. *American Psychologist, 34,* 1071–1084. (ERIC No. EJ 218 804)

Nicholls, J. G., & Jagacinski, C. (1983). Conceptions of ability in children and adults. Paper presented at the International Conference on Anxiety and Self-Related Cognitions, West Berlin, Germany.

Slavin, R. (1983). *Cooperative learning.* New York: Longman.

Weiner, B. (1979). A theory of motivation for some classroom experiences. *Journal of Educational Psychology, 71,* 3–25. (ERIC No. EJ 200 538)

IV

Social Comparison, Self-Efficacy, and Motivation

Dale H. Schunk

University of Houston

The purpose of this article is to discuss the role of social comparison in fostering a sense of self-efficacy and motivation in educational settings. *Social comparison* refers to the process of comparing oneself with others (Festinger, 1954). Such comparison is important because it affects students' motivation, learning, and perceived *self-efficacy,* or beliefs regarding their academic capabilities. Understanding the social comparison process can benefit preservice teachers in promoting student achievement.

Social comparison figures as an important influence on achievement behaviors in a variety of theoretical approaches (Ames, 1984; Bandura, 1981; Ruble, 1983; Schunk, 1984; Veroff, 1969). In achievement contexts, social comparison can enhance task motivation (Schunk, in press). These motivational effects are significant, because instructional procedures alone cannot fully account for students' diverse achievement patterns (Schunk, 1984). Social comparison can also inform students that they are capable of acquiring skills. As students then work at a task and observe their progress, their sense of capability is substantiated and helps to sustain motivation. Collectively, enhanced motivation and perceptions of capabilities (i.e., self-efficacy) promote skill development and may lead to further social comparisons.

At the same time, the effect of social comparison on achievement behaviors depends on students' ages and levels of function, because students' use of social comparative information changes over the course of development. The impact of social comparison also depends on the situation and on the characteristics of those to whom students compare themselves. For example, perceived similarity to others can moderate the effects of social comparison. Students who compare themselves with peers of similar ability may feel motivated to perform as well as their peers, whereas those who compare themselves with peers of much higher ability may become demoralized because they cannot perform as well and, as a result, may work halfheartedly on tasks. In short, how social comparison affects students' academic work depends on developmental and environmental factors.

SOCIAL COMPARISON: THEORY AND DEVELOPMENT

In everyday life, social comparison is an important source for learning what behaviors are appropriate (Masters, 1971; Veroff, 1969). Where absolute standards of behavior are ambiguous or nonexistent, acceptability of behavior is relative to what is practiced generally. For example, students who converse too loudly with one another in the school library are apt to be told by the teacher to work quietly. To convey acceptable behavior to the students, the teacher could point out others in the library who are talking quietly or whispering.

Social comparison also can help individuals learn how capable they are at a task. One's capabilities often are defined relative to the accomplishments of others. Festinger (1954) discussed this aspect of social comparison as follows: "To the extent that objective, nonsocial means are not available, people evaluate their opinions and abilities by comparison respectively with the opinions and abilities of others" (p. 118). The student who wins the school spelling bee is likely to feel quite competent in spelling; however, the student's spelling excellence is relative to that of other students in the school.

Social comparison is employed regularly by adults in evaluating their capabilities (Suls & Miller, 1977), but how children utilize social comparative information for self-evaluative purposes is less well understood. Developmental evidence suggests that the ability to use comparative information depends on higher levels of cognitive development and experience in making comparative evaluations (Veroff, 1969). Children younger than ages five or six are characterized by what Piaget termed *centration*, or the tendency not to relate two or more elements in thought, and *egocentrism*, which refers to the *self* dominating one's cognitive focus and judgments (Flavell, 1963; Higgins, 1981). These two characteristics do not mean that very young children cannot evaluate themselves relative to others; rather, they do not automatically do so. Children show increasing interest in comparative information in the early elementary school years, and by the fourth grade utilize such information to help evaluate their performance capabilities (Ruble et al., 1980; Ruble, Feldman, & Boggiano, 1976). Other research shows that by the fourth grade, students' performances on both motor and learning tasks are influenced by the performances of peers; however, the behaviors of younger children are affected more by direct adult social evaluation, such as praise ("You're doing well") and criticism ("You could do better") (Spear & Armstrong, 1978).

Research suggests that, although very young children engage in social comparison, the meaning and function of comparative information change with development and especially as a result of entering school. Preschool children actively compare at an overt physical level; they frequently compare the rewards they receive with those of others (Masters, 1971; Ruble et al., 1980). Mosatche and Bragonier (1981) found that preschoolers' social comparisons with peers primarily involved those instances of (a) establishing similarities to and differences from others ("I'm four and one-half, you're four; we both had a birthday"), and (b) competition based on a need or desire to be better than others but that does not involve self-evaluation ("I'm the general; that's higher than the captain"). Much less frequently, children engaged in social comparison to evaluate their qualifications ("I can do it, too").

Ruble and her colleagues (Ruble, 1983; Ruble, Feldman, & Boggiano, 1976) discuss the development of social comparison in young children as a multistep process. The earliest comparisons primarily involve similarities and differences, but then shift to a concern with how to do something. Feldman and Ruble (1977) found that first graders engaged in much peer comparison during an achievement task, but their primary purpose was to obtain correct answers. Thus, providing comparative information to preschoolers and children in primary grades may increase their motivation for more practical reasons (e.g., to obtain correct answers) than for acquiring information about personal capabilities (Ruble, Feldman, & Boggiano, 1976). It is important for preservice teachers to realize that young children do not necessarily become more motivated by being aware that others are performing better. At the same time, telling young children who fail at a task that most other children also do poorly may not alleviate the negative impact of failure (Ruble, Parsons, & Ross, 1976). After first grade, interest increases in determining how well peers are doing, and children use comparative information more often to evaluate their performance capabilities.

SOCIAL COMPARISON AND ACHIEVEMENT BEHAVIORS

A useful framework for relating social comparison to achievement behaviors is Bandura's social learning theory (Bandura, 1977b). According to this theory, behavior is in part a function of perceived *self-efficacy*, which refers to personal judgments of one's performance capabilities in a given activity (Bandura, 1977a, 1981, 1982).

Self-efficacy can influence students' choices of activities (Bandura, 1977a). Students who wonder whether they can accomplish a task may attempt to avoid it, whereas those who feel more capable should participate more eagerly (Schunk, 1984). Self-efficacy also can affect task motivation (Bandura, 1977a; Schunk, 1984). Especially when facing obstacles, students who feel more capable of succeeding should expend greater effort and persist longer than those who doubt their capabilities (Bandura & Schunk, 1981; Schunk, 1984). Students can learn about their capabilities through their actual performances, vicarious (observational) means, forms of persuasion, and physiological indexes (e.g., heart rate).

Social comparison of one's performance with the performances of others constitutes a vicarious (observational) means of deriving self-efficacy information (Bandura, 1981). There is evidence that similar others, rather than those much higher or lower in ability, offer the best information for judging one's own performance capabilities (Bandura, 1981; Suls & Miller, 1977). Once students begin to engage in social comparison for self-evaluation, perceived similarity is based more on actual performances than on underlying constructs such as ability, because it is not until around age nine that children begin to form a distinct conception of ability (Nicholls, 1978; Suls & Sanders, 1982). Telling children that similar others can perform a task ("See how well Shawn is doing") can promote self-efficacy for succeeding, because children are likely to believe that if such similar others perform at a certain level, they can as well. In contrast, comparing oneself with those performing either much better or much worse offers less information about what one can do. Preservice teachers need to realize, however, that as students become older they do increasingly judge perceived similarity in terms of underlying constructs such as ability (Davidson & Smith, 1982).

When students perceive their own performances to be lower than those of similar others, they are apt to believe that they can perform as well and become motivated to attain the comparative level (Masters, 1971). As students work at the task, motivation and self-evaluation exert reciprocal effects. Motivation leads to progress toward the comparative level. As students observe that they are making progress, their initial self-efficacy is likely to be substantiated (Schunk, 1984). Enhanced self-efficacy helps to sustain motivation. Collectively, these two processes result in higher skill development which can serve as the basis for further social comparisons.

As an example of this process, it is not unusual for elementary school children to experience some anxiety and to doubt their capabilities to execute gymnastic movements such as cartwheels or somersaults. Such children may benefit from observing peers performing these exercises. This observation may convey that peers can learn the exercises and motivate students to try them. Then, as children actually perform cart-

25

wheels and somersaults, they ought to notice that they are improving and not injuring themselves, which helps to sustain motivation. With skill improvement, children are apt to engage in further social comparison to determine how smooth their movements are compared with those of others.

The preceding discussion suggests that social comparison can affect students' motivation and convey information about their capabilities. Research bearing on these two issues is described below.

Motivational Effects

Research supports the idea that social comparative information can exert strong motivational effects on students' performances by the fourth grade (Schunk, 1983a; Spear & Armstrong, 1978). Feldman and Ruble (1977) also found an enhanced level of motivation among second graders compared with younger children. Within this context, certain factors influence the likelihood and effects of social comparison.

One theoretically relevant factor is an *objective standard for evaluation* (Festinger, 1954); that is, there ought to be greater interest in social comparison in the absence of an objective criterion against which to evaluate one's performance. Among third graders, Pepitone (1972) found that the presence of a correct finished product (e.g., a jigsaw puzzle) reduced social comparisons; however, among first and fourth graders, Feldman and Ruble (1977) obtained only a weak effect on interest in social comparison due to the absence of an objective performance criterion (e.g., a time standard for the best performance). Even when an objective performance criterion is present, students still may be interested in social comparison to assess their performance capabilities against those of others.

A second important factor is the *presence of competition;* social comparison theoretically should become more prevalent in a competitive setting. Although there are some exceptions, research studies generally have found increased comparisons in more-competitive as opposed to less-competitive or noncompetitive settings (Ames, 1981; Feldman & Ruble, 1977; Mithaug, 1973; Pepitone, 1972; Ruble, Feldman, & Boggiano, 1976). For example, Feldman and Ruble (1977) found increased interest in social comparison when children knew that only the first child to finish puzzles would win a prize. In short, competition appears to increase students' motivation to compare themselves with others.

The effects of *sex differences* also have been explored. Ruble, Feldman, and Boggiano (1976) obtained evidence that among children in kindergarten through second grade, boys showed greater interest in comparative information than girls. Spear and Armstrong (1978) found that comparative information exerted motivational effects on boys' performances on easier tasks, but not on difficult ones; no differences due to type of task were obtained for girls. Ruble, Feldman, and Boggiano (1976) suggest that there may be more societal pressure placed on boys than on girls to evaluate themselves relative to others.

Informational Effects

Students who adopt comparative information as a standard of performance ought to develop higher self-efficacy while working at the task and observing their progress toward the standard. Although research supports this proposition, the effects of comparative information on capability self-evaluations (i.e., self-efficacy) are not particularly strong. Schunk (1983a) provided comparative information to fourth graders on the typical progress of other similar children during a long division competency-development program. The comparative information enhanced motivation in that children demonstrated a high rate of problem solving during the training program, but the effect on self-efficacy for solving division problems was only modest. Ruble, Parsons, and Ross (1976) worked with children ranging in age from four to eleven on a matching familiar figures task (Zelniker et al., 1972). Children's affective reactions to the task and self-evaluations of ability were influenced more by task outcome (success or failure) than by comparative information indicating the difficulty of the task (easy or hard). Schunk (1983b) found that directly telling fourth graders that they could work a given number of problems during a division training program ("You can work twenty-five problems") enhanced children's self-efficacy more than providing comparative information indicating that other similar children could work that many problems.

Ruble, Parsons, and Ross (1976) state that providing students with comparative information leads to high interest in self-evaluation. Results of the Schunk (1983a, 1983b) studies suggest that in the absence of comparative information, students may focus on how their present performance attainments surpass their prior accomplishments, which seems to enhance self-efficacy more than comparisons with others.

What social comparative information conveys to students about their academic capabilities depends on the characteristics of the comparison students. When people compare themselves to similar others on ability-related attributes, they expect to perform at an equivalent level (Goethals & Darley, 1977). If their performance matches the comparative standard, they may not feel overly capable if they realize that their performance was only average (Schunk, 1983a). For most students, similar others are peers of average ability. Comparative information indicating average achievement motivates students to reach the standard, but may not promote strong self-efficacy. On the other hand, providing high achievers with performance information about other high achievers could promote high self-efficacy if students attain the comparative level.

At the same time, comparative information indicating average accomplishments conveys the clearest information to most students about their own capabilities. Information indicating an easy task ("All students can do this") conveys ambiguous information about one's capabilities (Goethals & Darley, 1977), because students who match the standard might nonetheless wonder how good they are. Conversely, comparative information indicating a difficult task ("Few students can do this") could stifle motivation because many students will be reluctant to attempt the impossible, and if their subsequent performances were worse than the comparative level, it would be unclear how capable they really were.

As an illustration, suppose that students were assigned twenty spelling words on Monday, study each day, and are tested on Thursday. Those who score 100 percent receive free time during Friday's spelling period, whereas others are retested on Friday. Students would learn little about their spelling capabilities if everyone scored 100 percent on the Thursday tests, because they probably will believe that the words were easy. On the other hand, few students would be motivated to put forth extra effort on studying during the week if hardly anyone scored 100 percent on the Thursday tests. Students could derive the clearest information about their own capabilities if about half of the class demonstrated mastery on Thursdays, because they could readily determine their relative standing (i.e., top or bottom half).

In short, comparative information indicating average performance is motivating for most students, but may not constitute the most effective means of enhancing capability self-evaluations. Again, directly informing students about their capabilities ("You can do this") may motivate them equally well but better enhance self-efficacy (Schunk, 1983a). Once students work at a task, their actual successes and failures become more important influences on their beliefs about their capabilities than peer comparisons (Ruble, Parsons, & Ross, 1976).

SOCIAL COMPARISONS IN THE CLASSROOM

Students frequently compare themselves with their classmates. Although such comparisons may exert motivational effects and convey some information about capabilities, a problem is that students may compare themselves with inappropriate others (i.e., those much higher or lower in competence). Students who compare themselves with superior others are apt to become demoralized when their attainments consistently fall short of the comparative levels, whereas students who compare themselves with those much lower in competence may overestimate what they can do and attempt tasks beyond their means.

28

Teachers frequently provide students with social comparative information ("Shawn, see how well Kevin is working"). Teachers who fail to select comparative others judiciously run the risk of students perceiving the comparative others as dissimilar to themselves. If Shawn believes that Kevin always works better than he does, this type of comparative information is not likely to improve Shawn's working habits.

Even if teachers carefully select comparative others and students perceive the comparative others as similar to themselves, it is necessary that students' subsequent performances at least approximate the comparative level if enhanced motivation and self-efficacy are to be sustained. Students who perform well below the comparative level suggested by the teacher may believe they are not particularly skillful and that further efforts will not lead to improvement.

As suggested earlier, an alternative to conveying social comparative information is to provide students with direct attainment information, such as, "I know you can do this" (Schunk, in press). Direct attainment information motivates students to work at a task (Schunk, 1983b). In the absence of comparative information students ought to focus on how their present performance accomplishments surpass their prior attainments; this focus builds self-efficacy (Schunk, in press). Students' actual successes and failures then become important influences on their evaluations of their capabilities (Ruble, Parsons, & Ross, 1976).

A related alternative for teachers is to suggest short-term goals to students ("Try to finish three pages by the end of the period"). Suggesting a goal to students conveys that they possess the necessary capabilities to attain it, which enhances motivation (Schunk, 1984). Progress towards a short-term goal is easy to gauge; therefore, students' initial self-efficacy for goal attainment is likely to be validated as they work at the task and observe their progress (Schunk, in press). In turn, higher self-efficacy helps to sustain task motivation and leads to further skill improvement. As students become more familiar with the task demands, they can set their own performance goals with teacher assistance as necessary.

Educational practices are important influences on motivation and self-efficacy (Schunk, 1984). It is important for preservice teachers to realize that educational practices also can affect social comparisons. Some examples of these effects are discussed below.

Reward Structures

How rewards are distributed in classrooms can influence students' social comparisons (Ames, 1981, 1984; Johnson & Johnson, 1974, 1975). Under competitive conditions, the opportunity for a student to receive a reward is reduced when others are successful. Competitive reward structures increase social comparisons (Ames, 1984). Such comparisons are apt to sustain motivation and lead to high self-efficacy among high achievers, because their performances will surpass those of others. The remaining students might become discouraged when they realize that they will not earn a reward, which could stifle motivation and lead to low self-efficacy for performing well.

In contrast with competitive structures, individualistic structures are characterized by rewards based on self-improvement; students' achievements are independent of one another and the opportunity for receiving a reward is equal across all students. Individualistic structures should be more likely to foster motivation and lead to higher self-efficacy among all students assuming that they perceive that their present performances exceed their prior attainments.

A third type of structure is characterized by cooperation such that group members share in the rewards based on their collective performance. Research shows that cooperative learning can reduce social comparisons, enhance students' beliefs about their capabilities, and convey to students that their efforts lead to success (Ames, 1981; Slavin, 1983). As such, the large differences between students in motivation and capabilities which are evident under competitive conditions, do not emerge.

Teachers who utilize individualistic and cooperative reward structures can help to minimize negative social comparisons. However, motivation and self-efficacy may suffer when students perceive no progress under individualistic conditions, and differences between students in motivation and evaluations of capabilities can emerge when cooperative groups are unsuccessful or when group rewards are not based on individual members' learning (Ames, 1984; Slavin, 1983). Preservice teachers need to learn to plan activities such that students will experience at least modest success under these conditions.

Modeling

Modeling is a form of social comparison (Schunk, in press). Observing others can motivate students and enhance self-efficacy because students may believe that if others can succeed they can as well (Bandura, 1981). This sense of efficacy is validated when students subsequently perform the task themselves and experience some success. Modeling is commonly employed by teachers during instruction.

Models who are similar to student observers offer the best basis for comparison (Rosenthal & Bandura, 1978). Perceived similarity may be based on personal attributes (e.g., sex, age, ethnicity), prior experiences, or perceived competence (Bandura, 1971; Schunk, in press). These considerations question whether teacher modeling really has much effect on students' self-efficacy, especially among low achievers who perceive the teacher as superior in competence.

To the extent that students perceive peer models as more similar to themselves, such models ought to promote students' motivation and self-efficacy better than teacher models. Further, because initial student learning often is fraught with difficulties, it may be that peer models who demonstrate coping behaviors would be especially effective. A distinction can be drawn between mastery and coping models. Mastery models demonstrate faultless performance from the outset, whereas coping models begin by demonstrating the typical errors and fears experienced by observers, but gradually improve their performance and gain self-confidence (Rosenthal & Bandura, 1978). Coping models illustrate how determined effort and positive self-thoughts can overcome difficulties. Research shows that coping models can enhance subsequent performance by observers more effectively than mastery models, and that modeled self-confidence can promote children's self-efficacy (Meichenbaum, 1971; Zimmerman & Ringle, 1981).

These considerations suggest that preservice teachers might be taught how to employ student peer models more often and incorporate coping behaviors into their own modeled demonstrations, particularly with students who may encounter difficulties mastering a task. Although both mastery and coping models convey skills, coping models are superior in promoting students' motivation and self-efficacy.

Tutoring

Tutoring is often used with remedial students because it provides the opportunity for greater student and individual feedback (Wagner, 1982). Although research shows that tutoring is an effective instructional strategy, it does not always promote student achievement better than group instruction (Cloward, 1967; Feldman, Devin-Sheehan, & Allen, 1976; Sindelar, 1982).

Tutors can affect students' social comparisons and confidence in their abilities (Wagner, 1982). Social comparison is apt to be minimized when students are tutored by adults. Under these circumstances, which actually constitute a type of individualistic reward structure, students are apt to focus on their academic progress. This type of focus should promote self-efficacy. Social comparisons should occur when peers (i.e., cross- or same-age) are utilized as tutors. The present article suggests that students are apt to feel more capable when they perceive tutors as somewhat similar to themselves, because students may believe that if tutors could master the skills, they can as well. Although teachers often select high ability students to tutor remedial ones, this type of arrangement may not promote students' self-efficacy as well as if they perceive their tutors' abilities as more similar to their own.

31

PRESERVICE TEACHER TRAINING

There are many ways that teachers can effectively use social comparative information to promote students' achievements about their capabilities, and teacher educators can incorporate these techniques into the normal coursework and activities engaged in by preservice teachers. During lesson planning, for example, preservice teachers can be given information about individual students (e.g., case studies) and can plan activities so that students not only experience success but also become aware of their progress in skill development. Preservice teachers can be instructed in how to convey progress feedback to students, such as with verbal feedback, log books, and progress charts.

Teacher educators can assist preservice teachers in determining how academic goals can be accomplished in different instructional formats and how to minimize negative social comparisons within those contexts. While developing lesson plans, for example, preservice teachers can be trained to consider alternative group formats (e.g., competitive, cooperative, individual). Although some tasks may lend themselves particularly well to one format, perservice teachers need to realize that grouping and reward structures often are left to their decision. Even after a format is selected, there are still decisions to be made. For example, how will the students become aware of their progress in an individualistic context? Will a cooperative group be successful? Teacher educators can assist preservice teachers address these concerns in their lesson plans.

Some of the ideas discussed in this article seem to lend themselves to role playing. Preservice teachers could be taught how to respond to inappropriate student social comparisons in a setting where one preservice teacher acts as the student and another acts as the teacher. For example, assume that Troy says to the teacher, "Aaron is better at math than I am." Teachers could help refocus Troy's attention to his own progress in math over the past few weeks by highlighting problems that Troy can work now that he could not solve previously.

It is likely that preservice teachers will need explicit training in how to incorporate peer modeling and tutoring into their instructional activities and in how to select models and tutors. Role playing also may be useful in this regard; preservice teachers could act as teacher and student. In mathematics, for example, the teacher could explain and demonstrate the appropriate operations, and then have the student model solve problems. With low achieving students, using a coping model may be highly appropriate. Initially, the model would encounter difficulties, but eventually would experience greater success. In working with a coping model, it is important that the teacher provide sufficient assistance so that the model succeeds while simultaneously emphasizing how the model's efforts are helping him or her learn. This type of peer modeling could be incorporated into various teaching methods courses so that preservice teachers learn how to integrate peer modeling with instruction on different subjects.

CONCLUSION

Recent research has shown that data derived from social comparisons can either enhance or deflate students' sense of self-efficacy, which in turn affects motivation. Since social comparisons are inevitable, in the classroom and in life, it seems sensible to structure classroom situations so as to maximize positive impacts of such comparisons on self-efficacy and motivation. For young children, direct assurance that they can accomplish a task may foster confidence more readily than comparative data about others. Research indicates that classrooms structured on individualisitc or cooperative models, as opposed to competitive patterns, are more likely to enhance feelings of self-confidence. Modeling, especially by similar others who exhibit coping behaviors, also ought to have a salutory effect. It is important for preservice teachers to be apprised of current theory in achievement motivation and to receive training in classroom strategies based on these concepts.

References

Ames, C. (1984). Competitive, cooperative, and individualistic goal structures: A motivational analysis. In R. Ames & C. Ames (Eds.), *Research on motivation in education: Student motivation* (Vol. 1). New York: Academic Press.

Ames, C. (1981). Competitive versus cooperative reward structures: The influence of individual and group performance factors on achievement attributions and affect. *American Educational Research Journal, 18,* 273–287. (ERIC No. EJ 253 000)

Bandura, A. (1971). Analysis of modeling processes. In A. Bandura (Ed.), *Psychological Modeling* (pp. 1–62). Chicago, IL: Aldine-Atherton.

Bandura, A. (1982). Self-efficacy mechanism in human agency. *American Psychologist, 37,* 122–147.

Bandura, A. (1977a). Self-efficacy: Toward a unifying theory of behavioral change. *Psychological Review, 84,* 191–215. (ERIC No. EJ 161 632)

Bandura, A. (1981). Self-referent thought: A developmental analysis of self-efficacy. In J. H. Flavell & L. Ross (Eds.), *Social cognitive development: Frontiers and possible futures* (pp. 200–239). Cambridge, England: Cambridge University Press.

Bandura, A. (1977b). *Social learning theory.* Englewood Cliffs, NJ: Prentice-Hall.

Bandura, A., & Schunk, D. H. (1981). Cultivating competence, self-efficacy, and intrinsic interest through proximal self-motivation. *Journal of Personality and Social Psychology, 41,* 586–598.

Cloward, R. D. (1967). Studies in tutoring. *Journal of Experimental Education, 36,* 14–25.

Davidson, E. S., & Smith, W. P. (1982). Imitation, social comparison, and self-reward. *Child Development, 53,* 928–932. (ERIC No. EJ 271 622)

Feldman, N. S., & Ruble, D. N. (1977). Awareness of social comparison interest and motivations: A developmental study. *Journal of Educational Psychology, 69,* 579–585.

Feldman, R. S., Devin-Sheehan, L., & Allen, V. L. (1976). Children tutoring children: A critical review of research. In V. L. Allen (Ed.), *Children as teachers: Theory and research on tutoring* (pp. 235–252). New York: Academic Press.

Festinger, L. (1954). A theory of social comparison. *Human Relations, 7,* 117–140.

Flavell, J. H. (1963). *The developmental psychology of Jean Piaget.* New York: D. Van Nostrand.

Goethals, G. R., & Darley, J. M. (1977). Social comparison theory: An attributional approach. In J. M. Suls & R. L. Miller (Eds.), *Social comparison processes:*

Theoretical and empirical perspectives (pp. 259–278). Washington, DC: Hemisphere.

Higgins, E. T. (1981). Role taking and social judgment: Alternative developmental perspectives and processes. In J. H. Flavell & L. Ross (Eds.), *Social cognitive development: Frontiers and possible futures* (pp. 119–153). Cambridge, England: Cambridge University Press.

Johnson, D. W., & Johnson, R. T. (1974). Instructional goal structure: Cooperative, competitive, or individualistic. *Review of Educational Research, 44,* 213–240.

Johnson, D. W., & Johnson, R. T. (1975). *Learning together and alone.* Englewood Cliffs, NJ: Prentice-Hall. (ERIC Document Reproduction Service No. ED 104 868)

Masters, J. C. (1971). Social comparison by young children. *Young Children, 27,* 37–60. (ERIC No. EJ 043 672)

Meichenbaum, D. H. (1971). Examination of model characteristics in reducing avoidance behavior. *Journal of Personality and Social Psychology, 17,* 298–307.

Mithaug, D. (1973). The development of procedures for identifying competitive behavior in children. *Journal of Experimental Child Psychology, 16,* 76–90.

Mosatche, H. S., & Bragonier, P. (1981). An observational study of social comparison in preschoolers. *Child Development, 52,* 376–378.

Nicholls, J. G. (1978). The development of the concepts of effort and ability, perception of academic attainment, and the understanding that difficult tasks require more ability. *Child Development, 49,* 800–814.

Pepitone, E. A. (1972). Comparison behavior in elementary school children. *American Educational Research Journal, 9,* 45–63. (ERIC No. EJ 051 478)

Rosenthal, T. L., & Bandura, A. (1978). Psychological modeling: Theory and practice. In S. L. Garfield & A. E. Bergin (Eds.), *Handbook of psychotherapy and behavior change: An empirical analysis* (2nd ed., pp. 621–658). New York: Wiley.

Ruble, D. N. (1983). The development of social-comparison processes and their role in achievement-related self-socialization. In E. T. Higgins, D. N. Ruble, & W. W. Hartup (Eds.), *Social cognition and social development* (pp. 134–157). New York: Cambridge University Press.

Ruble, D. N., Boggiano, A. K., Feldman, N. S., & Loebl, J. H. (1980). Developmental analysis of the role of social comparison in self-evaluation. *Developmental Psychology, 16,* 105–115.

Ruble, D. N., Feldman, N. S., & Boggiano, A. K. (1976). Social comparison between young children in achievement situations. *Developmental Psychology, 12,* 191–197. (ERIC No. EJ 139 800)

Ruble, D. N., Parsons, J. E., & Ross, J. (1976). Self-evaluative responses of children in an achievement setting. *Child Development, 47,* 990–997.

Schunk, D. H. (In press). Children's social comparison and goal setting in achievement contexts. In L. G. Katz (Ed.), *Current topics in early childhood education* (Vol. 6). Norwood, NJ: Ablex.

35

Schunk, D. H. (1983a). Developing children's self-efficacy and skills: The roles of social comparative information and goal setting. *Contemporary Educational Psychology, 8*, 76–86. (ERIC No. EJ 275 582)

Schunk, D. H. (1983b). Goal difficulty and attainment information: Effects on children's achievement behaviors. *Human Learning, 2*, 107–117.

Schunk, D. H. (1984). Self-efficacy perspective on achievement behavior. *Educational Psychologist, 19*, 48–58.

Sindelar, P. T. (1982). The effects of cross-aged tutoring on the comprehension skills of remedial reading students. *Journal of Special Education, 16*, 199–206.

Slavin, R. E. (1983). *Cooperative learning.* New York: Longman.

Spear, P. S., & Armstrong, S. (1978). Effects of performance expectancies created by peer comparison as related to social reinforcement, task difficulty, and age of child. *Journal of Experimental Child Psychology, 25*, 254–266. (ERIC No. EJ 183 933)

Suls, J., & Miller, R. C. (1977). *Social comparison processes: Theoretical and empirical perspectives.* Washington, DC: Hemisphere.

Suls, J., & Sanders, G. S. (1982). Self-evaluation through social comparison: A developmental analysis. In L. Wheeler (Ed.), *Review of personality and social psychology* (Vol. 3, pp. 171–197). Beverly Hills, CA: Sage Publications.

Veroff, J. (1969). Social comparison and the development of achievement motivation. In C. P. Smith (Ed.), *Achievement-related motives in children* (pp. 46–101). New York: Russell Sage Foundation.

Wagner, L. (1982). *Peer teaching: Historical perspectives.* Westport, CT: Greenwood Press.

Zelniker, T., Jeffrey, W. E., Ault, R., & Parsons, J. (1972). Analysis and modification of search strategies of impulsive and reflective children on the Matching Familiar Figures Test. *Child Development, 43*, 321–337. (ERIC No. EJ 059 510)

Zimmerman, B. J., & Ringle, J. (1981). Effects of model persistence and statements of confidence on children's self-efficacy and problem solving. *Journal of Educational Psychology, 73*, 485–493. (ERIC No. EJ 253 048)

V

Achievement Motivation and The Preservice Teacher

M. Kay Alderman
University of Akron

Although the need for Achievement as a theory of motivation has been described and researched since the 1950s, there is little evidence that it has been included in preservice programs to the extent that the preservice teacher has been able to apply its principles in the classroom. The purpose of this article is to establish a rationale for achievement motivation theory as an essential tool for the preservice teacher. (Throughout this paper, the terms achievement motivation, need for Achievement, *n*Achievement will refer to the theory of motivation, while the terms high achievement/achievers will refer to external measures such as standardized achievement scores.) This discussion assumes that it is as important to work on the motivation of the preservice teacher as it is the content knowledge base. The rationale will be established by identifying motivational characteristics of successful teachers; refocusing the content of achievement motivation to an emphasis on strategies used by individuals with high *n*Achievement and on the training for these strategies; and drawing parallels between characteristics of high need achievement individuals and successful teachers. Finally, suggestions will be offered for implementing achievement motivation in teacher education courses.

MOTIVATION AND THE SUCCESSFUL TEACHER

Research in effective teaching and effective schools has identified characteristics and strategies of successful teachers that have a motivational dimension (Brophy, 1983; Brophy & Evertson, 1976; Brook-

37

over et al., 1979; Good & Brophy, 1984; Good, Grouws & Ebmeier, 1983). From these research findings and concomitant recommendations for teaching, characteristics have been gleaned that appear to overlap with those of persons who exhibit high levels of achievement motivation.

Brophy and Evertson (1976) have concluded from their studies that one of the most fundamental variables in effective teaching is the instructor's role definition. The differences in successful and unsuccessful teachers on this variable were clearly motivational. Successful teachers perceived teaching as a worthwhile challenge and took personal responsibility for the progress of their students. Although they perceived that there were learning problems, they believed these could be overcome. In contrast, unsuccessful teachers were more likely to respond to student learning problems by giving up and attributing failure to outside causes; these teachers explained their failure in ways that allowed them to avoid the assumption of personal responsibility. Brophy and Evertson have concluded that the difference was not in the presence or absence of problems but in the ways teachers responded to them. Successful teachers responded with behaviors designed to overcome problems, while the less successful teachers attempted to shift responsibility to factors outside of their control, such as student attitudes and the administration.

Other studies have also identified characteristics of effective teachers that have motivational implications. From research on mathematics teaching, Good (1983) has described characteristics associated with effective mathematics instruction known as "active teaching." These teachers were more assertive in presenting and explaining concepts; provided appropriate practice activities and monitored those activities prior to seatwork; and looked for ways to confirm or disconfirm that their presentations had been comprehended by students. Similar to findings by Brophy and Evertson (1976), successful teachers assumed partial responsibility for students' learning and appeared ready to reteach if necessary. Furthermore, Brookover et al. (1979) found that teachers in high achieving black and white schools had this same acceptance of responsibility for student achievement. The teachers demonstrated this by spending much time discussing ways of improving achievement and reaching particular students, and provided reinstruction when students did not do well on assignments. They also went to other teachers for suggestions and were willing to meet with principals, students, or parents to discuss ways to increase student achievement.

Differences between more and less effective teachers have also been found in the area of expectations (Brookover et al., 1979). More effective teachers believed that higher achievement was a reasonable and attainable goal. They set achievement goals for students based on what was felt to be appropriate for the student grade level—not in terms of social class or family background—and then provided students with ways of achieving them. At the same time, the teachers were cognizant of problems associated with lower socioeconomic backgrounds and took these into account. In contrast, teachers in the lower achieving schools did not express concrete achievement goals and did not seem to accept responsibility for student attainment of goals. Good and Brophy (1984) have recommended that expectations should not be unrealistically high, but rather should be appropriate for the level of student ability.

The characteristics of successful teachers identified by the above researchers appear to be more than pedagogical skills. They represent a motivational profile which might be termed personal agency or teacher efficacy—that is, teachers believe they have the capacity to affect student performance (Ashton, 1983).

The student, as well as the teacher, has an active role in the successful classroom (Wittrock, 1979). Classroom research has identified several student characteristics that contribute to an effective instructional climate. Students should have the ability to evaluate their own work (Good & Brophy, 1984), and also to set goals and in turn monitor their performance (Brophy, 1983). Marx and Winne (1983) cite the need for students to acquire a positive motivational set in order to regulate their own learning. The assumption is that these are motivational characteristics to be acquired by students in the instructional process.

At this point, a motivational link is established between teacher and student. The effective teacher should have a sense of personal effectiveness or personal agency and motivated students are self-regulated learners. The question arises as to whether this personal agency is something that can be acquired, as teaching skills can, and in turn be transferred to students. In a paper identifying teacher competencies for the future, Marx and Winne (1983) suggest that teachers should be well-versed in motivational areas such as personal agency, as motivation theory should be part of the universal subject matter to be taught to students. It is suggested that the medium for doing this already exists through the context of achievement motivation training.

ACHIEVEMENT MOTIVATION: A REFOCUS

Although the need for achievement has been one of the most widely researched motives since the 1950s and is included in the motivation chapter of any undergraduate educational psychology text, its potential applicability in preservice education has hardly been tapped. The typical presentation is focused more on resultant achievement motivation (Atkinson, 1964) than on a description of the nAchievement syndrome and strategies and behaviors of individuals with nAchievement (McClelland & Winter, 1971). Although reports of achievement motivation training studies would be of utmost importance to prospective teachers, many texts either omit or mention only briefly the training projects by Kolb

(1965) and deCharms (1976). Gage and Berliner (1984) include one of the more extensive discussions of need for achievement as a theory of motivation, but omit any specific recommendations on how a teacher can apply this theory. Based on a survey of motivation chapters in undergraduate texts, it was concluded that the typical presentation of achievement motivation is totally inadequate to expect any application by the beginning teacher (Alderman, 1982).

A specific purpose of this paper is to refocus the presentation of achievement motivation from what has traditionally been included in the undergraduate text to a study of strategies used by persons who show high *n*Achievement patterns and the training for these strategies. The patterns of thinking about achievement and the strategies used by high *n*Achievement persons are essential to developing motivation in the preservice teacher.

The Achievement Syndrome

The achievement motive is most often defined as "success in competition with some standard of excellence" (McClelland et al., 1953, p. 80). A distinguishing characteristic of achievement motivation is that there is an achievement frame of reference involving standards of excellence in tasks. The crucial element of this frame of reference is that the individual demonstrates personal involvement in evaluating his/her performance in terms of the standard of excellence. "Whether the performance be grooming, playing football, landing a job, or herding sheep, it can give evidence of an achievement motive if there is affect or involvement connected with evaluation of it" (McClelland et al., 1953, p. 80). More specifically, the *n*Achievement syndrome includes a *desire* to reach an achievement goal, anticipation of *success* in attaining the goal or *failure* in not attaining it, *instrumental activity* designed to accomplish the goal, and anticipation of *blocks*, either *world* or *personal*, that could interfere with goal attainment.

Behavioral Characteristics of Achievement-Oriented Persons

Research indicates that there are a number of characteristics that differentiate persons with high and low need for achievement. These are considered not only characteristics of the person, but strategies used by persons with high *n*Achievement.

1. **Excellence/Urge to Improve.** They are interested in excellence for its own sake rather than for the rewards it brings. They try to perform well when measured by some standard of excellence. Their conversation is likely to be sprinkled with talk about "improving," "doing well," "doing something unique." They work

harder when there is a chance personal efforts will make a difference in the outcome, when there is a challenge, and where tasks have some degree of "mental manipulation" (McClelland, 1961).

2. **Personal Responsibility.** They tend to prefer situations in which they can take personal responsibility for the outcome of their efforts in order to maximize the likelihood of satisfaction from achievement (McClelland & Winter, 1971).

3. **Moderate Risk Takers.** They tend to set moderately difficult goals for themselves, neither too hard nor too easy so that they might derive more achievement satisfaction (McClelland & Winter, 1971).

4. **Concrete Feedback.** They are more likely than others to want concrete feedback on how well they are doing. The concrete feedback also allows them to keep track of progress toward their goals. They prefer work situations where they can tell easily whether they are improving or not. They want to know if an act is instrumental in solving problems (McClelland, 1978).

5. **Researching the Environment.** Persons with high nAchievement approach new situations with initiative and engage in exploratory behavior. They continually research the environment to find tasks they can solve to their satisfaction and generally try out more new things. The high nAchievement person wants to find out the "rules of the game," and make sure he/she knows what is going on and what options are open. They are more active (McClelland & Winter, 1971).

The successful teachers described earlier have characteristics that are strikingly similar to characteristics of high nAchievers. A summary of these similarities is found in Table 1.

The most important point is that there are training techniques to develop achievement motivation. Thus, achievement motivation training is a possible vehicle for fostering the motivational attitudes found in successful teachers.

ACHIEVEMENT MOTIVATION TRAINING

One of the strongest arguments for making achievement motivation theory part of the curriculum for the preservice teacher is that we know a great deal about specific training procedures to develop achievement motivation. Although the specific training components may vary somewhat in length and in whether they are taught separately or integrated into subject matter content in school, the aim of the training is to teach the person to think, talk, and act like a person with high nAchievement patterns.

Table 1

Similarities Between Achievement Motivation Factors and Successful Teachers

Achievement Motivation Factors	Successful Teachers
Expressed desire to reach achievement goal	Set achievement goals for students
Concern for excellence	Believe higher achievement a reasonable goal
Assumption of personal responsibility for outcomes	Take personal responsibility for learning of students
Willingness to take moderate risks	Set expectations appropriate to student ability
Desire for concrete feedback	Confirm or disconfirm student comprehension
Need to research environment	Spend time discussing ways of improving achievement and reaching particular students; meet with principal, student, or parents to discuss ways to increase achievement; seek suggestions from peers
Perception of blocks	Perceive learning problems associated with lower socioeconomic background, but believe these can be overcome
Perserverence and persistence	Willing to reteach if necessary
Instrumental activity	Provide ways for students to obtain goals; provide reinstruction; present concepts actively

Motivation Training in Schools

The best known and most extensive accounts of motivation training in the schools are the projects by Alschuler (1973) and deCharms (1976). The two projects utilized different approaches to training. The Alschuler or Harvard project gave brief intensive training directly to school children, while the deCharms approach first trained teachers who in turn trained their students. The deCharms project also included personal causation training which was designed to help individuals feel more like an *origin* (causing own behavior) than a *pawn* (powerless over circumstances). The deCharms project involved the following kinds of activities for teachers: *self-study* of their own motives and how they could increase their motivation so they might understand better the motives of others (This process was begun by having each participant write an essay on, "Who Am I?"); *realistic goal setting* for themselves in their classrooms (A ring toss game is used to teach realistic goal setting.); development of *concrete plans* to reach their goals; *evaluation* of progress toward reaching their goals. The two main aspects of the training, according to deCharms (1976), were personal responsibility and planning of concrete action.

The motivation training component for students was integrated with the content area. Classroom exercises included: self-study or activities designed to foster development of self-concept; achievement motivation thinking; realistic goal-setting; and origin-pawn training to help students take charge of their own lives. One example of the training inputs was a "spelling game" which involved realistic goal-setting in which a student could choose between easy, moderate, or difficult words based on ability. Another example was storywriting about achievement and origin themes which was used in a classroom essay contest. (Full descriptions of the training are found in deCharms, 1976.)

The results of the study indicate that the motivation training had positive effects on the motivation of both teachers and students. The trend for low achieving students to fall increasingly further behind on standardized achievement scores was reversed for students who received the motivation training as compared to nontrained students. In addition, trained students showed less absenteeism and tardiness. DeCharms has drawn several conclusions from the project. First, the most effective training is that which enhances motivation in the context of academically relevant materials. Also, embedding motivation in subject matter exercises like the spelling game was highly successful. Finally, integrating motivation concepts, especially the connection between striving and goal attainment, into subject matter has enormous potential for education.

The Alschuler or Harvard motivation training project tried a number of methods in addition to the intensive courses taught directly to students (Alschuler, 1973; Alschuler, Tabor, & McIntyre, 1971). In some methods, classrooms were restructured so students were permitted more self-direction. In other methods, the motivation training was integrated with classroom work, while still others used mastery learning courses. McClelland (1972) reviewed the effects of the motivation training and concluded that the most effective method was the integration of the training with the classroom work. Equally important is the conclusion that restructuring the classroom for self-reliance without the formal instruction in achievement motivation had no effect on motivation or academic performance. McClelland has concluded on the basis of these projects that direct instruction in motivation is necessary.

The motivation training of the teachers was also linked to improved classroom management procedures. McClelland points out the overlap between teacher behaviors in origin classrooms in the deCharms (1976) project with the behaviors Kounin (1970) identified as important in highly involved classrooms. In highly involved classrooms, students were involved in work and free from deviant behavior. In both situations, important teacher variables were getting attention, insuring active participation, and making individuals feel accountable. It is important to note, however, a difference in the motivation training approach to classroom management and direct instruction models of teaching (Rosenshine, 1979). In direct instruction, the teacher is a strong leader who elicits attention and active participation from the students and closely monitors their work. In the origin trained classrooms, the teacher includes a component that would enable the student to become more effective in regulating his/her own attending, participating, and monitoring behavior.

More recently, Heckhausen and Krug (1982) have developed and tested other types of motivation training programs. These differ from those described above in that they are focused on a few individual aspects of motivational processes. The primary interest has been on achievement motivation as a self-evaluation system. Training programs have been directed toward helping children set more realistic goals and develop causal attributions that enhance their self-value. Additional training programs focused on changing teacher reference norms from social comparison, where teachers compared an individual student's performance in terms of the class average to an individual perspective which focuses more on the student's progress relative to his/her own base line. The findings were positive in that students exposed to individual reference norms used less social comparison (see the article by Schunk in this volume), had better performance on tests, and viewed their performance as successful.

It has been shown that successful teachers exhibit many of the same characteristics as persons who are described as having high nAchievement patterns. Achievement motivation training for teachers has been linked to increased learning by students. This suggests that not only is achieve-

44

ment motivation essential knowledge, it is essential motivation for the preservice teacher. Preservice teachers should know that they can facilitate motivation in the classroom.

ACHIEVEMENT MOTIVATION IN TEACHER EDUCATION

From the link between high *n*Achievement and motivation of successful teachers, two primary objectives for the preservice teacher are suggested. First, preservice teachers should be able to use achievement motivation to examine and understand their own motives; and second, they should be able to implement basic motivation strategies such as realistic goal setting. Perhaps there are a number of ways that these achievement motivation objectives could be accomplished in the preservice program. One possibility is the inclusion of motivation training as a clinical component. Another is to embed it in the course content. Cohen (1984) has described an educational psychology course that has taken the latter approach.

Two important points should be made regarding the accomplishment of the motivation goals. The first is that the teacher educator must understand both McClelland's and deCharms' approaches to motivation change. Second, the educator must know how to apply these approaches. As Karplus (1981) points out, the reason students cannot make applications is that we fail to provide them with sufficient examples. (See Appendix A for an example of an achievement motivation structure in a physical education class.) Also, as teacher educators apply these motivation strategies, they are modeling motivation application for preservice teachers.

From their experience in motivation training, McClelland and Winter (1979) concluded that no one of the various inputs is necessary or sufficient by itself. They suggested that the most important goal was to learn to think like a person with high *n*Achievement. In this context, the following are specific suggestions for embedding achievement strategies into course structures.

1. **Achievement motivation thinking and acting.** In achievement motivation training this is done by persons writing and scoring stories with achievement themes. The theme of a course in teacher education could be that successful teachers have a motivation set in terms of goals, expectations, and personal responsibility for learning outcomes. Thus, preservice students might begin to think like successful teachers. In addition, case studies of students and teachers with high *n*Achievement patterns both present and absent could be presented for diagnosis.
2. **Realistic goal-setting strategies, concrete feedback, and instrumental activity.** Preservce students could be asked to state

45

goals for the course and/or for each exam. This could be combined with instrumental activity by asking them to specify what they will do to accomplish the goal. They can monitor their work and acquire concrete feedback by keeping records of progress. In addition, students can be taught the criteria for evaluation so they can judge their own performances. There appear to be enormous possibilities for combining these strategies with metacognitive approaches which emphasize students' self-awareness and control of their own learning processes (Brown, Campione, & Day, 1981). For example, Brown (1978) recommends that students should be taught to "stop, check (self-test), and study if necessary."

3. **Researching the environment.** Before starting tasks like papers or projects, have preservice students discuss what is wanted and needed in the project and identify world or personal blocks that might interfere with successful completion.

4. **Understanding motives.** Simulation activities can be used to examine one's own motives, such as origin/pawn feelings. The author developed a brief version of the origin/pawn game for use in educational psychology classes. In one condition, students were free to construct something with tape, scissors, and colors; in a second condition, they constructed an object (turkey) by very rigid instructions. (Cohen, 1984, describes a different simulation for the origin/pawn experience.) The students wrote down all the adjectives they could think of to describe their feelings in each experience and shared these. Through this activity, preservice students are able to experience concretely how they and others are motivated differently by conditions of freedom and constraint.

Since there is little documentation about preparing preservice teachers in achievement motivation, Schools of Education need to try various approaches and begin to collect data on their effectiveness. A follow-up of participants in the author's achievement motivation workshops indicates that the strategy most applied by teachers is realistic goal-setting, both for themselves and their students. Thus, if one achievement strategy had to be chosen, it might be realistic goal-setting. Relevant research in goal-setting can be found in Gaa (1973); Bandura and Schunk (1981); and Bandura and Cervone (1983).

CONCLUSION

Teaching has not been thought of as an occupation where individuals with a high need for Achievement will find satisfaction since dimensions such as concrete feedback have been missing. It appears, however, that the nature of teaching as an occupation is changing. The findings from teaching effectiveness research are being used to specify teacher behaviors that are linked to increased classroom performance on achievement tests. These descriptions of effective teaching practices can be used to give teachers a framework for observing their own teaching behaviors (Good & Brophy, 1984). Thus, it becomes a medium for providing concrete feedback and self-evaluation.

When one examines the characteristics of high nAchievement behavior, it can be seen that teachers and students who possess them have an edge over those who do not. Two descriptive phrases that really capture this refocus of achievement motivation for preservice education are "the urge to improve" (McClelland & Winter, 1971) and "information seeker" (Weiner, 1980). These phases connote an image of a teacher that would be highly desirable in a climate where we seek to improve the quality of education and teaching. It is likely that the preservice teacher who has the "urge to improve" will become the "active teacher," and it is unlikely that "active teachers" will develop from passive learners in preservice education. It is important for teacher educators to know that there are training procedures to foster characteristics of high nAchievement, and it is important for preservice teachers to know there is potential for motivation change.

References

Alderman, M. K. (1982). Motivation in teacher education: Current trends and suggestions for essential knowledge. Paper presented at the annual meeting of Midwest Association of Teachers of Educational Psychology, Dayton, Ohio.

Alschuler, A. (1973). *Developing achievement motivation in adolescents.* Englewood Cliffs, NJ: Educational Technology Publications.

Alschuler, A., Tabor, D., & McIntyre, J. (1971). *Teaching achievement motivation: Theory and practice in psychology education.* Middletown, CT: Education Ventures.

Ashton, P. (1983). *A study of teachers' sense of efficacy.* Final Report, Executive Summary. Gainesville, FL: University of Florida. (ERIC Document Reproduction Service No. ED 231 833)

Atkinson, J. W. (1964). *Introduction to motivation.* Princeton, NJ: Van Nostrand.

Bandura, A., & Cervone, D. (1983). Self-evaluation and self-efficacy mechanisms governing the motivational effects of goal systems. *Journal of Personality and Social Psychology, 41,* 1017–1028.

Bandura, A., & Schunk, D. (1981). Cultivating competence, self-efficacy, and intrinsic interest through proximal self-motivation. *Journal of Personality and Social Psychology, 41,* 586–598.

Brookover, W., Beady, C., Flood, P., Schweitzer, J., & Wisenbaker, J. (1979). *School social systems and student achievement.* New York: Praeger.

Brophy, J. (1983). Classroom organization and management. In D. Smith (Ed.), *Essential knowledge for beginning educators.* Washington, DC: American Association of Colleges for Teacher Education. (ERIC Document Reproduction Service No. ED 237 455).

Brophy, J., & Evertson, C. (1976). *Learning from teaching: A developmental perspective.* Boston, MA: Allyn & Bacon.

Brown, A. L. (1978). Knowing when, where, and how to remember: A problem of metacognition. In R. Glaser (Ed.), *Advances in instructional psychology.* Hillsdale, NJ: Lawrence Erlbaum.

Brown, A., Campione, J. C., & Day, J. D. (1981). Learning to learn: On training students to learn from texts. *Educational Researcher, 10,* 14–21. (ERIC No. EJ 241 605)

Cohen, M. W. (1984). Enhancing motivation in educational psychology. *Teaching of Psychology, 11,* 214–217.

Cohen, M. W. (1982). Using motivational theories as a focus for the educational psychology curriculum. Paper presented at the annual meeting of the Midwest Association of Teachers of Educational Psychology, Dayton, Ohio.

deCharms, R. (1976). *Enhancing motivation.* New York: Irvington/Wiley.

deCharms, R. (1968). *Personal causation.* New York: Academic Press.

Gaa, J. P. (1973). Effects of individual goal-setting conferences on achievement, attitudes, and goal-setting behavior. *The Journal of Experimental Education, 42,* 22–28.

Gage, N. L., & Berliner, D. C. (1984). *Educational psychology* (3rd ed.). Boston, MA: Houghton-Mifflin.

Good, T. L. (1983). Recent classroom research: Implications for teacher education. In D. Smith (Ed.), *Essential knowledge for beginning educators.* Washington, DC: American Association of Colleges for Teacher Education. (ERIC Document Reproduction Service No. ED 237 455).

Good, T. L., & Brophy, J. E. (1984). *Looking in classrooms* (3rd ed.). New York: Harper & Row.

Good, T. L., Grouws, D. A., & Ebmeier, H. (1983). *Active mathematics teaching.* New York: Longman. (ERIC Document Reproduction Service No. ED 242 798)

Heckhausen, H., & Krug, S. (1982). Motive modification. In A. J. Stewart (Ed.), *Motivation and society.* San Francisco, CA: Jossey-Bass.

Karplus, R. (1981). Education and formal thought: A modest proposal. In I. Sigel, D. Brodzinski & R. Golinkoff (Eds.), *New directions in Piagetian theory and practice.* Hillsdale, NJ: Lawrence Erlbaum Associates.

Kolb, D. A. (1965). Achievement motivation training for underachieving high-school boys. *Journal of Personality and Social Psychology, 2,* 783–792.

Kounin, J. S. (1970). *Discipline and group management in classrooms.* New York: Holt, Rinehart, and Winston.

McClelland, D. C. (1961). *The achieving society.* New York: Free Press.

McClelland, D. C. (1978). Managing motivation to expand human freedom. *American Psychologist, 33,* 201–210. (ERIC No. EJ 176 751)

McClelland, D. C. (1972). What is the effect of achievement motivation training in the schools? *Teachers College Record, 74,* 129–145. (ERIC No. EJ 067 531)

McClelland, D. C., Atkinson, J. W., Clark, R. A., & Lowell, E. L. (1953). *The achievement motive.* New York: Appleton-Century-Crofts.

McClelland, D. C., & Winter, D. G. (1971). *Motivating economic achievement.* New York: Free Press.

Marx, R. W., & Winne, P. H. (1983). Knowledge and skills teachers need to influence students' cognitive learning. Paper presented at annual meeting of American Educational Research Association, Montreal, Quebec.

Rosenshine, B. (1979). The third cycle of research on teacher efforts: Content covered, academic engaged time, and direct instruction. In P. Peterson & H. Walberg (Eds.), *Research on teaching: Concepts, findings, and implications.* Berkeley, CA: McCutchan.

Weiner, B. (1980). *Human motivation.* New York: Holt, Rinehart and Winston.

Wittrock, M. C. (1979). The cognitive movement in instruction. *Educational Researcher, 8,* 5–11. (ERIC No. EJ 197 331)

Appendix A

Achievement Motivation Structure of a Physical Education Class

The following is a description of a senior high school girls' physical education class in a middle-class neighborhood. There are five classes for a total of approximately 250 students.

Activity	Achievement Motivation Strategy
On the first day of class students completed a self-evaluation of their health and physical fitness status, competence level, interest in the various activities, and then set goals for the year.	SELF-STUDY; GOAL SETTING
Weekly self-tests were given in all types of physical fitness, i.e., flexibility, strength and posture. Each student recorded scores in a team notebook.	SELF-STUDY; CONCRETE FEEDBACK
At the end of the first nine-week grading period, students set goals for final exam based on the feedback from the self-tests. Each student was asked to set what seemed to her to be a realistic goal. There were a variety of ways students could	GOAL-SETTING

accomplish the aerobic goal, i.e., job, walk, jump-rope. After goals were set, the instructor met individually with each student to discuss whether the goals were realistic (most were).

Each student established a practice schedule of three times a week for the nine-week term. The practices were recorded on individual record cards. (This step was added the second year after it was found students did not practice consistently.)

INSTRUMENTAL ACTIVITY; CONCRETE FEEDBACK

After final exam, students completed self-evaluation on what they learned.

SELF-STUDY

To the instructor, the most striking comment made by students on the final self-evaluation was, "I learned to set a goal and accomplish it."

VI

Motivational Coursework in Teacher Education

Mary Rohrkemper

Bryn Mawr College

Although most teacher education curricula include knowledge of research and theory about student motivation, such content information is not sufficient motivational training for preservice teachers. In addition to motivational content knowledge, preservice teachers need *process* skills to enable them to diagnose the need for motivational strategies; assess the effectiveness of strategy implementation; and fine-tune or modify implemented strategies as indicated by the assessment process. Within this framework the teacher is viewed as an information processor and decision maker. As in other areas of classroom practice and research, there are no cookbook approaches to successful motivation in the classroom. It is possible however, to design a curriculum that provides education students with heuristic skills that will help them decide if, when, and how to implement prescriptions derived from both research and practice.

TEACHER EFFECTIVENESS RESEARCH

Research on teacher effectiveness and decision making in the area of classroom management, in particular, can be helpful in constructing such coursework. An interrelationship between teacher management skills (typically measured by frequency, intensity, and duration of inappropriate student behavior) and end of the year student achievement has been found consistently in these investigations (Good, 1973, 1983; Good & Brophy, 1980). Thus, teachers who are effective managers also tend to be effective instructors. This relationship between managerial and instructional skill is probably due to the fact that teachers who are more effective classroom managers have to face less inappropriate student behavior in the first place, and consequently have a greater proportion of class time available for instruction. The more effective classroom manager, then, is able to increase both the time students are engaged in their work and the amount of time spent on actual instruction, both of which are associated with improved student achievement (Fisher et al., 1978; Good & Grouws, 1979; Rosenshine, 1979, 1980).

With a few exceptions (Slavin, 1983), the role of appropriate motivational systems in the relationship between classroom management and instruction has not been specifically addressed. Rather, it has typically been assumed, or at best limited to discussions of appropriate level of task difficulty (meaning high success rates). As such, this research does not directly address motivation in the classroom. This literature does, however, inform motivational behavior through the emergence of the concepts of proactive and reactive decision making.

PROACTIVE AND REACTIVE DECISION MAKING

The linkage between management and instructional skill in the teacher effectiveness research can be tied to an underlying, pervasive teacher behavior that has been termed "proactive." Proactive teacher behavior indicates an active decision making process that is characterized by a positive goal orientation (versus mere control/desist goals); deliberate planning (versus nonreflective habit or reaction); and a preventive focus (versus remedial orientation). Proactive teacher behavior is based on a philosophical framework that includes the expectation that students can, and will, learn, and that the teacher is key to the arrangement of that learning.

In contrast, reactive decision making and instruction refer to those teacher behaviors that occur in the "interactive" (Shavelson, 1976) or ongoing phase of instruction in response to unanticipated events. Reactive instruction primarily involves teacher *response* to student behavior that is seen as inappropriate, and thus is usually viewed from management rather than instructional perspectives.

Reactive decisions and instruction differ from proactive decisions and instruction in terms of the amount of time available for decision making and the timing of the subsequent strategy. In reactive instruction the time available for assessment of the situation and construction of an appropriate strategy is brief and the event is already in progress. Thus, the likelihood of misdiagnosis of the situation and less than optimal teacher response is greater than in the proactive mode.

The interrelationship between proactive and reactive instruction is evident. The more proactive decision making and behavioral strategies that a teacher engages in, the more predictable the classroom environment becomes, thereby decreasing the need for reactive decision making.

Proactive behavior in general, then, increases the ability to anticipate possible problem spots associated with particular subject matter, lesson formats, and individual students (Morine-Dershimer, 1979). As such, the need to respond to unexpected student behavior is markedly reduced.

DECISION MAKING IN THE
MOTIVATIONAL DOMAIN

The distinction between proactive and reactive teacher decision making and behavior that has emerged from the teacher effectiveness literature has much to offer those interested in teacher motivational behavior. In this context, *proactive motivational behavior* would be based on a belief that students can and will be motivated to learn and participate as members of the class, and that the teacher is key to such motivation. This philosophy would be reflected in teacher instructional decisions, targeted to groups of students and individuals, designed to enhance motivation. These decisions would include, for example, proportion of "successful" problems in seatwork and planned novelty in question sequence during direct instruction. Group level motivational decisions include, for example, the use of cooperative groups or competitive games, and task presentation statements such as "this will be on the test," or "this unit is important" or "fun." Decision making in dealing with students on an individual basis is reflected in strategies to enhance individual efficacy, particularly in new and independent learning, and contingency contracts to increase performance.

Similarly, *reactive motivational behavior* would include those motivational teacher strategies that occur in response to perceived need during the course of classroom instruction, and may be targeted to the group or to individuals. For example, the teacher may adjust instructional plans to include "high success" review questions in response to student frustration with new or difficult material. Reactive decision making may also involve rethinking use of public praise statements if students appear uncomfortable due to embarrassment or irritation.

Finally, reactive decisions in response to individual students would be tailored to specific problems, so that an underachiever not doing an assignment would be treated differently from a student perceived as not working because of uncertainty or fear. As in the teacher effectiveness research, a relationship between proactive and reactive motivational behavior can be anticipated. That is, the more appropriate and flexible the proactive motivational system, which includes decisions and strategies stemming from instructional concerns (group and individual), the less likely would be the need to respond to student motivation problems in each of these domains.

Teacher Self-Awareness

Successful proactive and reactive motivational decisions and strategies are based on the teacher's awareness both of *self* and of *students*, so that what is communicated to students is what the teacher intended. For example, if a teacher wishes the classroom goal structure to be an individualistic one (tied to individual self-improvement independent of others' performance), yet the reward, accountability, or even decorating system includes posting student papers, students may perceive teacher intention as one of fostering student achievement through competition (in quantity and quality of displayed papers). Such perceptions increase the likelihood that students will engage in potentially detrimental social comparison, an outcome the teacher had sought to avoid and would be hard pressed to predict and thus appropriately respond to given the intended motivational decisions and goals.

Concern with teacher self-awareness is particularly important in those domains in which the instructor has vested interests, such as a commitment to particular instructional goals or highly valued socialization concerns. Self-interest can bias the natural attributional process (Weiner, 1979) of making sense of one's social environment. For example, Brophy and Rohrkemper (1982) found that teachers who perceived themselves as relatively more concerned with the instructional aspects of the teacher role reported more irritation with students who did not live up to their academic potential compared with other troublesome students. Similarly, teachers who perceived socialization of students as the more important aspect of their role as classroom teachers reported more frustration with students who were hostile toward others than with other types of difficult students.

In the classroom, teachers need to be aware not only of their attributions about student motivation, but also of how these attributions affect teacher beliefs about their own efficacy and subsequent strategies for motivating students. For example, work by Brophy and Rohrkemper (1981) and Rohrkemper and Brophy (1983) indicated that students perceived by their teacher as not doing assignments because they did not want to (as opposed to being forgetful, fearful, or unable to) were correctly assessed as acting intentionally and capable of doing otherwise. Teachers were pessimistic about their ability to meaningfully change these students, and reported treating them in ways that would not be likely to foster more appropriate student motivation. These strategies would also probably decrease student response to future extrinsic motivational attempts. This pattern points to the need for teachers to be aware of ways in which they may unwittingly support dysfunctional motivational patterns among certain students. Self-monitoring is required if appropriate motivational decision making is to occur.

55

Student Perceptions

Even though teachers may carefully examine their own intentions and behavior, they cannot assume their students share these perceptions and concerns. Because teaching is a social process, accurate communication can only be assured when teachers are aware of their students' understanding of teacher expectations and behavior. Too often teachers mistakenly assume they share an understanding with students. Teachers' awareness of perceptions that students are *likely* to have can be increased by encouraging integration across coursework in instructional and cognitive psychology, social psychology, and child social-cognitive development as teachers engage in proactive motivational decisions.

For example, given the findings of motivational research, teachers can expect that the nature of rewards—their saliency (Lepper & Greene, 1978), contingency criteria (quality or quantity), and informative value (Deci, 1976)—plays an important role in motivational effectiveness. In addition, teachers can expect students to respond differently to rewards in terms of learning, performance, and attitude as a function of several factors. These include student prior learning (Condry & Chambers, 1978), task characteristics (McGraw, 1978), and developmental level (Brophy, 1981). Developmental concerns in particular play a role in student response to the public or private aspects of teacher reward attempts and in student understanding of the relationship between motivation and learning. Young students do not view ability and effort in the same manner as do older students or adults (Wittrock, in press).

Motivational Skills Training

The ability to use this knowledge of students and tasks (the "contents" of motivational coursework) relies on a working knowledge of assessment and monitoring skills (the "process" components of motivational coursework). These skills enable the teacher to determine if teacher proactive motivational goals have been met, and, if found wanting, to implement remedial strategies to attain these goals (reactive motivational decisions and behavior).

Evaluation of the effectiveness of reactive decisions and strategies, including both intended and unexpected effects, also requires assessment skills. For example, monitoring for potential unintended effects of student attribution retraining, in which emphasis was placed on ascriptions to effort to increase task persistence, would lead a teacher to discover if student time on task increased (the intended effect). The assessment process would also disclose if student time away from other, more readily successful, tasks also increased. A potential unintended effect, then, could be that student performance in one domain precluded student growth in other domains. In this scenario, the ultimate result, student loss of a profile (i.e., multifaceted) self-view and concomitant increased unidimensional (low ability student) self-view, may not, in fact, facilitate future learning. Discovery of a total effect, then, is only possible if the teacher is taught to monitor for the *un*intended as well as the intended outcome of motivational decisions and strategies with individual students and the classroom group.

Educating teachers in these process skills would involve training to increase self-awareness and to develop strategies for monitoring students. Three methods for assessing motivation should be included in the undergraduate curriculum: observation, class discussion, and interview.

Observation Strategies

Group Monitoring. It is necessary to become aware of one's "perceptional blinders" (Good & Brophy, 1978) in order to learn from observation rather than merely verify or justify prior notions. For example, when examining the effectiveness of praising Sally, who has been especially productive today, the teacher should look not just for Sally's continued productive behavior (intended), but also for effects on Sally's classmates who witness her praise (potentially unintended). Do the onlookers appear envious? Intimidated? Irritated? Has the teacher praised Sally at the expense of appearing unfair to the rest of the class? Has the teacher inadvertently portrayed Sally as the "teacher's pet" and made her a target of ridicule by her peers? Such unintended effects invite devisive coalitions among students and between teacher and students. Group monitoring, then, helps the teacher gauge the full range of effects of motivational strategies with a single student or group of students.

Target Student Monitoring. Closer, more intensive monitoring can be facilitated with systematic record keeping. An Antecedent-Behavior-Consequence formula would help teachers attend to contextual factors and student behavior that may mediate teacher motivational goals. Thus, teachers can keep records of the type of situation in which the student typically exhibits motivational difficulty (the antecedents of the behaviors), the behavior the student usually engages in that indicates motivational problems (the behavior), and teacher and peer responses to that behavior (the consequences). For example, Antecedent-Behavior-Consequence recordkeeping helps a teacher notice that when Bill is given the entire set of math seatwork to be completed by the end of the day, he does not get started. Instead, he shuffles and re-shuffles papers and sharpens his pencil and straightens his desk. His constant movement annoys his classmates seated near him who eventually make derogatory comments. Bill in turn attempts to save face. Awareness of this scenario enables the teacher to implement reactive decisions to help Bill acquire the ability to engage in large amounts of work without becoming overwhelmed. In addition, assessing student interpretation of teacher motivational strategies will aid in generating hypotheses about behavior that can be shared with the student through individual conference or class discussion. Thus, in the above example the teacher inferred that Bill was overwhelmed by the amount of work that he was given. This inference, or hypothesis, about the cause of Bill's behavior can be shared with Bill to rule out the other explanations (such as the work is too easy and Bill knows he can get it done in the 5 minutes before it is due, or the work is too hard and Bill cannot do any of it no matter how much time is given, or Bill does not know how to get along with his classmates and tries to get their attention during class). The teacher can then provide the rationale underlying his/her response to Bill (e.g., why it is important for the development of self-regulation, the importance of a smooth-running classroom to support everyone's learning). Verification is important. Although much is gained from careful observation, it cannot guarantee correct interpretation of what is seen, nor accurate communication of what is expected.

Verbal Report Strategies

Techniques for verifying observed patterns of individual and group behavior include class discussion and individual student interviews. Systematic observation followed by discussion and/or interview encourages teacher and student to assess their attempts to understand one another. Teachers benefit from increased knowledge about student perceptions; the effectiveness of teacher communication of expectations and motivational goals; and the congruence between teacher goals and motivational decisions and behavior.

Class Discussion. The special benefit of classroom discussion—that is, providing exposure to a range of perceptions and gaining awareness of the subjective nature of interpersonal understanding—has been discussed elsewhere (Bessel & Palomares, 1967; Glasser, 1969). However, the efficacy of classroom meetings as forums where teachers can learn about students' expectations and gauge how well their behavior is reinforcing these should be stressed. A nonthreatening, nonjudgmental atmosphere is crucial in successful (i.e., "valid") class discussions (Glasser, 1969).

Interview. Interviewing techniques are essential in training teachers how to gather the information necessary to assess the effects of their motivational decision making. Much student motivational life occurs "inside of the head," and as such is not directly understood through observation. Thus, obtaining information from students that can inform decision making will often require an individual interview.

Recommendations for a curriculum in interviewing can be drawn from research efforts to interview children (Cannell & Kahn, 1968; Wein-

58

stein, 1980; Wolf, 1979; Yarrow, 1960). As argued elsewhere by this author (Rohrkemper, 1982), the interview is first and foremost a social process. The teacher's stance as a concerned and interested adult, always needed in the classroom, is critical to the quality and validity of individual student interview data. Data is invalid to the degree that the information provided does not reflect students' true feelings and thoughts. Teacher biases and expectations may lead to distortion in student reports. Such distortions may be elicited by the framing of the question ("Why did you do that?" versus "Tell me what happened."), or by the teacher's manner (blaming, supporting, or neutral). The presence of consequences the student may wish to obtain or avoid, such as teacher approval or punishment, may also skew the results of the interview.

Obviously, not all presentation effects can be controlled. However, we can train our education students to be aware of the demand characteristics of their speech, to identify appropriate times to interview students depending on the kind of knowledge they seek, and to recognize factors that may interfere with the validity of students' reports (Rohrkemper, 1982). (See also Cannell & Kahn, 1968; Ericsson & Simon, 1980; and Nisbett & Wilson, 1977 for discussion of validity issues in obtaining and interpreting verbal reports.) Given these potential constraints, there is nonetheless much that can be learned through the careful use of interviews about the effectiveness of teacher motivational (and instructional) decisions and strategies, student understanding of teacher intention and expectations, and student attitudes toward one another and the teacher.

One rule of thumb to increase the probability that information is an accurate reflection of the student's thoughts and is consistent on subsequent occasions is to interview stuents after they have "calmed down." When students are removed from a situation it is likely that they will have time to reflect on their experience; this may improve their insight and enable them better to report their perceptions. Students' reports are more likely to be reliable after some initial "distancing." However, reliability does not always serve validity. When concerned with how the student feels when in a situation, immediacy takes precedence.

Yarrow (1960) delineates many considerations in constructing and conducting interviews. For instance, he relates the degree of structure in a question with the type of responses that are desired ("Do you understand why I want you to finish all of the assignment? vs. "How can you help me decide if you need help with this assignment or if you understand it really well?" vs. "What are some things that students could do so teachers know how well they are learning?"). Yarrow also discusses direct, indirect, and projective questions. While direct questions effectively elicit factual information, indirect questions are better when information about complex student attitudes, feelings, and expectations is desired. For example, if a teacher is concerned about a particular student's lack of interest in social studies, the teacher may choose to ask the student indirect questions based on observation of the student's behavior and an analysis of what is involved in a social studies lesson. The teacher might ask: "Of reading, math, and social studies, which do you like most (dislike least)?" And again, "If you could choose to read quietly, have a class discussion, or have me lecture, which would you choose first? What next?" and so on, to narrow down what it is about social studies that interferes with the student's work habits.

Projective questions involve the use of hypothetical situations (into which students "project" themselves) that help uncover in a nonthreatening way students' perceptions of teacher behavior and intention. For example, after a failure-syndrome student has read a story about a child who fears failure, ask, "How do you think the boy in the story felt when he was going to learn something new?" A student's anxiety can also be reduced by suggesting that others have felt the same way the student does, or by mentioning a variety of feelings or actions that people share, without attaching preference to any. A teacher might ask, "Everybody gets bored sometimes. I've noticed that some kids get bored when the work's too hard, some when it's too easy, others get bored in some classes but not others, some kids only get bored during seatwork, others only in class discussion. What about you? When do you get bored? Why do you think that is? What do you do when that happens?" The teacher lets the student know that she or he is aware that everyone gets bored and that it is understandable. By providing a range of possible situations that could be boring, the teacher is more likely to put the student at ease and obtain valid information.

It is also important for teachers to identify the situation and their rationale clearly, so that students understand that the teacher is trying to obtain information and further understanding, and not trying to punish or moralize. It is important for teachers to establish a credible tone of interest and concern, but not one of evaluation or emotional release. Students need to understand their teacher's intentions in order to develop enough trust to share their perceptions. If students get the impression that this will come back to haunt them, resistance, face-saving, or ingratiation are apt to occur. The invalid information obtained under these circumstances does little to improve teacher-student relations and student motivation.

In summary, in addition to grounding teachers in motivation theory as applied to the classroom, it is also important to teach preservice teachers how to diagnose motivation problems, develop intervention strategies, determine the effects of those decisions, and revise strategies when needed. Instruction in how to obtain information in the classroom through observation and interview skills seems key to such assessment, decision making and re-evaluation.

EVALUATION

How can teacher educators know when they have met (or approximated) these goals? An appropriate testing and evaluation format would recognize that there are few, if any, motivational behaviors that teachers engage in that are guaranteed to succeed. While this makes standard definitional or multiple choice formats problemmatic, modifications readily can be made to facilitate measurement of teacher decision making, self- and student assessment in light of these decisions, and appropriate modification of behavior as needed. Such instruments would use written, audio, or video vignettes depicting a range of classroom events as the item stems, followed by decision-oriented questions that logically build upon student responses in each subsequent question. This type of branching decision-tree approach would distinguish the student's ability to make an initial reasoned decision from the ability to follow-up on that decision as needed. Students would score incorrectly not if they originally erred, but if they did not assess the effects of their decision and re-evaluate or alter their thinking and strategies when additional information indicated that this was needed. In this way, it would be possible to assimilate some of the complexity, spontaneity, and ambiguity of the classroom.

This type of test-taking would be an educative experience, since beginning teachers would be exposed to feedback concerning the effects of their decisions. Test-takers would become aware of the relationship between the effectiveness and flexibility of their own proactive motivational decision making and the necessity for reactive decisions as unanticipated motivational problems arise. The testing format advocated here, then, provides student teachers with a profile of their strengths and weaknesses in the domain of motivational decisions and process skills. It also is a tool to enhance their understanding of these processes. No single approach or "right" answer is sought. Evaluation, in addition to the educative component, consists of a minimum competency cut-off score to identify those teachers with serious misunderstandings of motivational processes. Those failing to meet the minimum competency would be required to take additional instruction as indicated by their diagnostic profile.

CONCLUSION

Research has found that some teachers are more effective than others and that effective proactive teacher behavior can be taught. It is also clear, however, that there are no universal, specific teacher behaviors that will always prove successful. Differences in contextual factors, including students, instructional goals, and subject matter, all restrict the ability to describe specific teacher behavior. The same is probably true of motivational teacher behavior. What can be provided in teacher education programs, however, is heuristic instruction in the "what" of motivational knowledge, and the "how" of implementing that knowledge. The teacher as an active information processor and decision maker filters general strategies and principles through the particular demands of the teaching context. Such filtering demands both levels of preparation.

References

Besell, H., & Palomares, U. (1967). *Methods in human development.* San Diego, CA: Human Development Training Institute.

Brophy, J. (1981). Teacher praise: A functional analysis. *Review of Educational Research, 51,* 5–32. (ERIC No. EJ 246 420)

Brophy, J., & Rohrkemper, M. (1981). The influence of problem ownership on teachers' perceptions of and strategies for coping with problem students. *Journal of Educational Psychology, 73,* 295–311. (ERIC No. EJ 253 016)

Brophy, J., & Rohrkemper, M. (1982). *Motivational factors in teachers' handling of problem students.* Research Series No. 115. East Lansing, MI: Michigan State University.

Cannell, C., & Kahn, R. (1968). Interviewing. In G. Lindzey & E. Aronson (Eds.), *Handbook of social psychology* (Vol. 2, 2nd ed.). Reading, MA: Addison-Wesley.

Condry, J., & Chambers, J. (1978). Intrinsic motivation and the process of learning. In M. Lepper & D. Greene (Eds.), *The hidden costs of reward: New perspectives on the psychology of human motivation.* Hillsdale, NJ: Erlbaum.

Deci, E. (1976). *Intrinsic motivation.* New York: Plenum Press.

Ericsson, K., & Simon H. (1980). Verbal reports as data. *Psychological Review, 87,* 215–251. (ERIC No. EJ 231 273)

Fisher, C., Filby N., Marliave, R., Cahen, L., Dishaw, M., Moore, J., & Berliner, D. (1978). *Teaching behaviors, academic learning time and student achievement.* Final Report of Phase III-B, Beginning Teacher Evaluation Study. San Francisco, CA: Far West Laboratory.

Glasser, W. (1969). *Schools without failure.* New York: Harper and Row.

Good, T. (1983). Classroom research: A decade of progress. Invited address presented at the annual meeting of the American Educational Research Association, Montreal, Canada.

Good, T. (1979). Teacher effectiveness in the elementary school: What we know about it now. *Journal of Teacher Education, 30,* 52–64. (ERIC No. EJ 205 612)

Good, T., & Brophy J. (1984). *Looking in classrooms* (3rd ed.). New York: Harper and Row.

Good, T., & Grouws, D. (1979). The Missouri Mathematics Effectiveness Project: An experimental study in fourth-grade classrooms. *Journal of Educational Psychology, 71,* 355–362. (ERIC No. EJ 208 799)

Lepper, M., & Greene, D. (1978). *The hidden cost of reward: New perspectives on the psychology of human motivation.* Hillsdale, NJ: Erlbaum.

McGraw, K. (1978). The detrimental effects of reward on peformance. In M. Lepper & D. Greene (Eds.), *The hidden cost of reward: New perspectives on the psychology of human motivation.* Hillsdale, NJ: Erlbaum.

Morine-Dershimer, G. (1979). *Teacher plans and classroom reality: The South Bay Study, Part IV.* Research Series No. 60. East Lansing: MI: Institute for Research in Teaching, Michigan State University.

Nisbett, R., & Wilson, T. (1977). Telling more than we know: Verbal reports on mental processes. *Psychological Review, 84,* 231–259. (ERIC No. EJ 163 657)

Rohrkemper, M. (1982). Teacher self-assessment. In D. Duke (Ed.), *Helping teachers manage classrooms.* Alexandria, VA: Association for Supervision and Curriculum Development.

Rohrkemper, M., & Brophy, J. (1983). Teachers' thinking about problem students. In J. Levine & M. C. Wang (Eds.), *Teacher and student perceptions: Implications for learning.* Hillsdale, NJ: Erlbaum.

Rohrkemper, M., & Good, T. (in press). Proactive instruction. In T. Husen & N. Postlehwaite (Eds.), *International encyclopedia of education: Research and studies.* London, England: Pergamon Press.

Rosenshine, B. (1979). Content, time, and direct instruction. In P. Peterson & H. Walberg (Eds.), *Research on teaching: Concepts, findings, and implications.* Berkeley, CA: McCutchan.

Rosenshine, B. (1980). How time is spent in elementary classrooms. In C. Denham & A. Lieberman (Eds.), *Time to learn.* Washington, DC: Department of Education.

Slavin, R. (1983). *Cooperative learning.* New York: Longman.

Shavelson, R. (1976). Teachers' decision making. In N. Gage (Ed.), *The psychology of teaching methods. The 75th yearbook of the National Society for the Study of Education. Part One.* Chicago, IL: University of Chicago Press.

Weiner, B. (1979). A theory of motivation for some classroom experiences. *Journal of Educational Psychology, 71,* 3–25. (ERIC No. EJ 200 538)

Weinstein, R. S. (1980). Interviewing students. Presentation at Michigan State University, East Lansing.

Wittrock, M. (In press). Student's thought processes. In M. Wittrock (Ed.), *Handbook of research on teaching* (3rd ed.). Washington, DC: American Educational Research Association.

Wolf, R. (1979). Strategies for conducting naturalistic evaluation in socio-educational settings: the naturalistic interview. Occasional Paper Series. Kalamazoo, MI: Evaluation Center, Western Michigan University.

Yarrow, L. (1960). Interviewing children. In P. Mussen (Ed.), *Handbook of research methods in child development.* New York: Wiley and Sons.

About The Authors

M. Kay Alderman is associate professor of Educational Foundations at the University of Akron. Her research interests include facilitating thinking and achievement motivation in preservice teachers. She teaches courses in Educational Psychology.

Carole Ames is associate professor of Educational Psychology at the University of Illinois. Her research focuses on the effects of competition and learning environments on the attributions that learners make. She teaches courses in Educational Psychology.

Margaret W. Cohen is assistant professor of Education at the University of Missouri-St. Louis. Her research interests include enhancing the motivation of preservice teachers and understanding the career development of teachers. She teaches courses in Educational Psychology.

Mary Rohrkemper is assistant professor of Human Development at Bryn Mawr College. Her research focuses on understanding how teacher and student perceptions influence classroom processes. She teaches courses in Educational Psychology.

Dale H. Schunk is associate professor of Educational Psychology at the University of Houston. His research interests include self-efficacy in achievement contexts and cognitive strategies employed during learning. He teaches courses in Educational Psychology.